ANNA YUDINA

MULTI VERSE

ART, DANCE, DESIGN, TECHNOLOGY
THE EMERGENT CREATION

DIANA VISHNEVA
FOUNDATION

5
CONTINENTS

This book has been initiated
and inspired by Diana Vishneva.

MULTI
VERSE

" In modern cosmology and quantum physics, MULTIVERSE is the hypo-

thetical collection of parallel universes, including our own, that together

comprise all of reality that exists: the entirety of space, time, matter and

energy as well as the physical laws and constants that describe them.

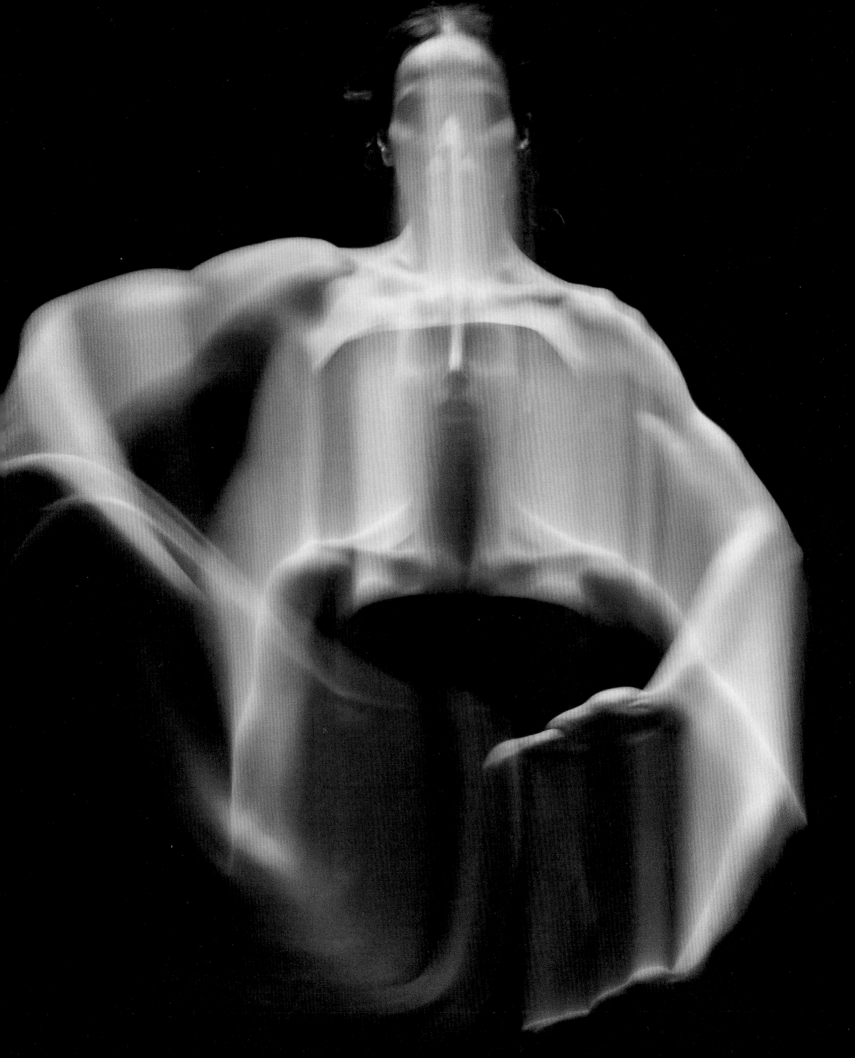

In this book, **MULTIVERSE** is an ever-expanding collection of parallel universes, in which a new universe is born each time a creative mind finds a unique way to share its vision.

DIANA VISHNEVA, praised by William Forsythe as one of the artists that "define the vector of their practice", combines the sublime skills of a classical ballet dancer with an ardent desire for experimentation. Past and ongoing collaborations with leading contemporary dance innovators—Maurice Béjart, Carolyn Carlson, Mats Ek, William Forsythe, Marco Goecke, Jirí Kylián, Edouard Lock, Hans van Manen, Ohad Naharin, John Neumeier, Moses Pendleton, Angelin Preljocaj—include pieces created specifically for Vishneva.

CARLO RATTI is a founding partner of the international design office Carlo Ratti Associati and director of Senseable City Lab at MIT. He was a TED speaker and curator of the Future Food District pavilion for the 2015 World Expo in Milan, and is currently serving as co-chair of the World Economic Forum Global Council on the Future of Cities and Urbanisation. His work has been exhibited at the Venice Biennale, the Science Museum in London, MoMA in New York and the Design Museum of Barcelona.

TOYO ITO is the founder of Toyo Ito & Associates, the recipient of the Golden Lion award for Lifetime Achievement at the 8. Architecture Biennale in Venice (2002) and the laureate of the 2013 Pritzker Architecture Prize. "Seeking to extend the possibilities of architecture," Ito was lauded by the Pritzker Prize jury as "a creator of timeless buildings, who at the same time boldly charts new paths," and "a true master who produces oxygen rather than just consumes it."

FRANCIS KURKDJIAN studied piano and classical ballet before venturing into fine perfumery. At 25, he created *Le Mâle*, the first men's fragrance by Jean Paul Gaultier, followed by over 40 perfumes for some of the world's best known brands including Christian Dior, Guerlain, Lanvin, Yves Saint Laurent. In 2001, he opened his pioneering bespoke perfume workshop. His own label, Maison Francis Kurkdjian, was born in 2009. Olfactory experiments for various artistic projects represent another facet of his work.

PHILIPPE RAHM expands architectural practice into the domains of physiology and atmospheric physics. He represented Switzerland at the 8. Architecture Biennale in Venice (2002) and was one of the 25 Manifesto architects selected by Aaron Betsky, the director of the 11. Architecture Biennale (2008). His work was exhibited at the Centre Pompidou, the San Francisco MoMA and the Guggenheim Museum, Mori Art Museum, Louisiana Museum, and at the Canadian Centre for Architecture (solo exhibition).

ANGELIN PRELJOCAJ, the leader of the Ballet Preljocaj who has authored works for the Paris Opera Ballet and the New York City Ballet, compares his approach to that of science as it requires both fundamental and applied research. Since 2000, he explores the dialogue between live dancers and digital imagery. He has created multimedia pieces for Karlheinz Stockhausen's *Helicopter String Quartet*, a trilogy based on John Cage's *Empty Words*, but also narrative ballets like *Romeo and Juliet* or *Snow White*.

JOHN NEUMEIER is the director and chief choreographer of the Hamburg Ballet since 1973, as well as the founder of the School of the Hamburg Ballet. As a choreographer, he focuses on preserving ballet tradition while developing a modern dramatic framework. This commitment manifests itself in the revised versions of the classical 'story ballets' and in the narrative forms created for his new works. Based on Neumeier's unique collection, his Foundation is a major resource for the research, documentation and presentation of dance.

ROSS LOVEGROVE is a pioneer of industrial design, winner of the World Technology Award for design (2005). He draws inspiration from "the logic and beauty of nature." Lovegrove's work is held in permanent collections by various design museums around the world, including MoMA in New York, Design Museum in London and Vitra Design Museum in Weil-am-Rhein.

IRIS VAN HERPEN fuses cutting-edge technologies with traditional couture craftsmanship to "blend the past and the future into a distinct version of the present." Her work is marked by collaborations with artists and architects and fuelled by an interest in science and technology. Six of her dresses have been acquired by New York's Metropolitan Museum of Art. She has created garments for Björk's videos and tours and collaborated with choreographers Benjamin Millepied and Sasha Waltz.

ENKI BILAL has played a major role in the evolution of contemporary comic books, a highly synthetic genre by nature. In 2012, he became the first comics artist to have a solo exhibition at the Louvre where he presented *The Ghosts of the Louvre* project. His multimedia installation *Inbox* was presented at the Venice Biennale in 2015. Bilal's work as a film director includes *Immortal* (2004), based on his graphic novel and being among the first major films shot entirely on a virtual backlot.

CARSTEN NICOLAI explores the transitional space between music, art and science as he makes natural phenomena like sound and light frequencies perceivable for both eyes and ears. He participated in major exhibitions such as documenta X and the 49. and 50. Venice Biennale. Like the musician Alva Noto he has collaborated with Ryuichi Sakamoto, Ryoji Ikeda, Blixa Bargeld and Mika Vainio and performed at the Guggenheim Museum, the San Francisco MoMA, Centre Pompidou and Tate Modern.

MARCO GOECKE's particular movement language has made him one of the world's most sought-after choreographers. Choreographer in residence of the Stuttgart Ballet and associate choreographer with Nederlands Dans Theater, Goecke has presented a remarkable number of world premieres in Stuttgart and NDT and has produced works for many renowned international companies including the Scapino Ballet Rotterdam, the Hamburg Ballet, Les Ballets de Monte Carlo and the Norwegian National Ballet.

BILL VIOLA has played a crucial role in establishing video as a vital form of contemporary art. He represented the US at the 46. Venice Biennale. In 2002, he completed his most ambitious project, a cycle of digital video 'frescoes', *Going Forth By Day*, commissioned by the Deutsche Guggenheim Berlin and the Guggenheim Museum, New York. In 2006–07, his exhibition at the Mori Art Museum in Tokyo attracted over 340,000 visitors. His two works, *Martyrs* and *Mary*, are permanently installed in St Paul's Cathedral in London.

 SANTIAGO CALATRAVA's works—many of which are bridges, major transportation hubs and cultural facilities—blend architecture, structural engineering and the fascination with nature-designed human and animal forms into highly expressive structures. Gravitational forces and the structural performance of materials are embodied in his dramatic sculptural designs.

 MIGUEL CHEVALIER is a pioneer of virtual and digital art who uses computer as his means of artistic expression. Among the recurrent themes explored in his works are nature and artifice, flows and networks, virtual cities and Islamic ornaments. Since the 1980s, Chevalier's primary field of research is the hybrid, generative and interactive image. His virtual reality installations use large-scale projections and are complemented by 3D-printed or laser-cut sculptures, and holographic imagery.

 AES+F work at the crossroads of photography, video and digital technologies. They achieved international recognition at the 52. Venice Biennale with the large-scale video installation, *Last Riot*. The subject of almost 100 solo exhibitions in some of the world's most prestigious cultural venues, their works can be found in the collections of the Moderna Museet, the Sammlung Goetz Museum, the Neue Galerie Graz, the Centre Pompidou, the Multimedia Art Museum Moscow, the Tretyakov Gallery and the State Russian Museum.

 EDOUARD LOCK, one of Canada's most internationally successful and innovative choreographers and the founder of the dance company La La La Human Steps, has created works for Cullberg Ballet, Het Nationale Ballet, Nederlands Dans Theater and Paris Opera Ballet. He has co-created and directed rock musician David Bowie's *Sound and Vision* world tour (1989), and collaborated with Frank Zappa, Einstürzende Neubauten, Kevin Shields (My Blue Valentine), David Van Tiegham, West India Company, David Lang and Gavin Bryars.

 MOSES PENDLETON is the founding member of the Pilobolus Dance Theater (1971), and founder and artistic director of MOMIX (1980). "I continue to be interested in using the human body to investigate non-human worlds," says Pendleton, who is reputed as one of America's most innovative choreographers for his company's highly inventive, phantasmagorical multimedia performances.

 AITOR THROUP is an artist, designer and creative director. Researching new ways of telling stories through object design, his multi-disciplinary studio collaborates across multiple industries and develops the conceptual clothing brand New Object Research. In 2010, Throup collaborated with Umbro to design the English national football team's 'away' kit for the World Cup. He made award-winning music videos as the creative director of British rock band Kasabian, and creatively directed Damon Albarn's debut solo album.

 OLAFUR ELIASSON's work is driven by his interests in perception, movement, embodied experience and feelings of self. He represented Denmark at the 50. Venice Biennale (2003) and exhibited his work at Tate Modern, San Francisco MoMA, MoMA New York, Louisiana Museum, Fondation Louis Vuitton, the Moderna Museet. Together with architect Sebastian Behmann, he founded Studio Other Spaces, an office for art and architecture focused on interdisciplinary, experimental building projects and works in public space.

 RAFFAELLO D'ANDREA is an engineer, new media artist and entrepreneur; professor of dynamic systems and control at the Swiss Federal Institute of Technology (ETH) in Zurich and founder of Verity Studios, creators of autonomous and interactive systems for entertainment. His work has been exhibited at the Venice Biennale, Ars Electronica, the Spoleto Festival, the Smithsonian, and is part of the permanent collections of the National Gallery of Canada, the FRAC Centre in France and the Heinz Nixdorf Museum in Germany.

 NICK KNIGHT's long-standing involvement with digital technologies has opened up new perspectives for both photography and fashion. He has collaborated with cutting-edge designers like Yohji Yamamoto, John Galliano, Alexander McQueen and directed music videos for Björk, Lady Gaga and Kanye West. He is the founder of the SHOWstudio website that has pioneered fashion film and became a unique cultural platform that shows "the entire creative process from conception to completion."

 WILLIAM FORSYTHE's works are featured in the repertoire of virtually every major ballet company, including the Mariinsky Ballet, New York City Ballet, San Francisco Ballet, National Ballet of Canada, Semperoper Ballet Dresden, England's Royal Ballet and the Paris Opera Ballet. His architectural and performance installations, or *Choreographical Objects*, have been presented in numerous museums and exhibitions, including the Whitney Biennial, the Louvre, Tate Modern, MoMA, ICA Boston and the Venice Biennale.

 CAROLYN CARLSON, the leader of the Carolyn Carlson Company, describes her choreography—which has been instrumental in the rise of French and Italian contemporary dance —as 'visual poetry'. In 2006, her work was rewarded with the first ever Golden Lion given to a choreographer by the Venice Biennale. She has been a resident artist and artistic director in Venice, Helsinki, Stockholm, the director of the National Choreographic Centre Roubaix Nord-Pas de Calais and a resident choreographer at the National Theater of Chaillot in Paris.

DIANA .. VISHNËVA

You say that you are always looking for the idea of a movement. What does that mean? Even as a young student, I wished my performance to become so convincing that, seeing Juliette or Tatiana, people would feel as if they were reading those lines from Shakespeare or Pushkin. I was blessed to have Valentina Kovaleva as my professor who taught me to search for the meaning of each movement and then fill it with spirit. This gave me strength to overcome countless obstacles. Simply perfecting technical skills is boring; it can boost my adrenaline levels, but will never inspire me unless I understand how to invest a movement with the right emotion—which, in return, transforms the movement itself, helping me to breathe life into my character._____ *But how does one fill a movement with meaning?* Every movement is justified by what you can tell through it. I'm not necessarily talking about lofty feelings; it can be as plain as showing how you react to someone calling you. You have to find the ultimately valid image that will be powerful, organic, spontaneous and convincing; hence the enormous effort, pain and time invested in this work. My mentor taught me to fill the gaps. She used to say: "Learn to *exist* in a pause, so that, even if you are doing nothing, the audience won't be able to take their eyes off you, because your stillness is meaningful, and they are appreciating this meaning." This doesn't mean that the spectator has to have the same thoughts as I do. I am not giving them a riddle to solve; it's my thought helping them to recognise their own thoughts or emotions._____ *I find the experiments of William Forsythe, whose artworks dissociate choreography from the human body, extremely interesting.* I see this as a research into movement as a universal language. From its early days on, classical ballet has been evolving towards increasing the sense of weightlessness, as if the dancers were floating above the stage. Contemporary dance explores

15

(facing) Giselle. *Choreography: Jean Coralli, Jules Perrot, Marius Petipa*

the metaphysics of the human body that seems to no longer have bones. You just can't understand how these movements are possible at all. William Forsythe has come a long way, but he had taken the classical structure as the starting point of his evolution, while, for instance, Mats Ek's choreography is rooted in the dramatic art. My first encounter with Martha Graham's style was a shock. It was the opposite of what a classical ballerina was supposed to do, but, once you mastered that style, you discovered the spiritual power of the woman. Love and tragedy in a classical ballet and in Graham's modern dance piece are treated in two completely different manners. Your self-consciousness changes, because, as your focus shifts to other body parts and muscles, you revise your entire 'artistic vocabulary'. Just like you grow into a role and can no longer distinguish yourself from your character, you can grow into a choreographic style, and this will transform you._____**I imagine that every new collaboration with a choreographer who is an innovator is like having to learn a new language.** No matter how professional a dancer you are, when you approach a different choreographic style, you immediately lose ground, because your entire operating system collapses. You go through physical and psychological withdrawal. Surrounded by the people who seem to move effortlessly because they have been practicing this for years, you feel helpless like an infant, but then you realise that you just have to reprogram your concepts; to force your body out of trying to perform those movements in habitual ways. Yet, accelerated learning is not enough; you have to thoroughly master the new style, otherwise you may carefully imitate the movements and still have *Swan Lake* written all over you . . . I'm not a fan of talking about my work. Anything I can say feels so flat compared to what I feel and discover when I dance._____**Non-verbal thinking at its purest?** I'm scared to even imagine what would have become of me without dancing. This is my way of educating and improving myself. You can say much more through dance. When words are

(above and page 269) <u>Subject to Change</u>, 2011. *Choreography: Paul Lightfoot & Sol Léon*

(below) <u>Subject to Change</u>, 2011. Choreography: Paul Lightfoot & Sol Léon
(pages 6 and 20) <u>Bolero</u>, 2011. Choreography: Maurice Béjart
(pages 22–3) <u>Vertigo</u>, 2010. Choreography: Mauro Bigonzetti

creativity

risk

rebellion

If your creative language consisted of words, what would the keywords be?

QUEST

lacking, just go and dance._____You speak about the state of inner rebellion that has largely shaped you as an artist . . . I love to challenge myself. Shaping my skills and my professional experience into something new; an opportunity to bring it together with other art forms to create something completely different—this is my biggest source of excitement today. I also love taking risks; trying something new rather than already tested, failsafe, and therefore boring. You won't be tempted by anything that is within reach, but finding a door to another dimension is thrilling._____New forms towards which art evolves today enrich and expand human perception, which becomes possible through joining forces with other disciplines, and not only artistic ones. This may feel disturbing at first, but is in fact an invitation to question our beliefs about reality. Thinking with your mind versus thinking with your body. How far is what we see from the 'real' reality? One goes from disorientation to realising how the world is immensely larger and more unpredictable than our concepts of it. Your work forms part of this process. No wonder you find it hard to describe it with words. It's a miracle that you are waiting to happen, and, once you've been there, your only goal is to experience it again. If your work becomes a routine, then the sense of wonder that has to be shared by both the artist and the spectator disappears . . . We can only see the

surface of the Earth, but not the magma, just like we don't see the underwater portion of an iceberg. In each artist, this 'iceberg' should be very strongly present. Sometimes people who come to the theatre for the first time in their life feel blown away. They may feel scared by having uncovered something about themselves they had never expected, but they will come back for further revelations. Again, words are too simple to convey what stands behind those revelations and how, in tiny steps, one develops an ability to move people._____**How do you find the right movement?** I do zillions of tests exploring one aspect, then shifting the focus towards something else. You collect and compare countless versions, but then you have to purify your collection. It's all about the degree to which you will be able to collect and purify, and no level of professionalism will secure you from turning into a set of cliches once you stop searching, because something that felt convincing yesterday may appear false today. _____Dance consists not only of movements, but also of transitions between them. Your *line of movement* has to be so powerful that it will leave the audience breathless, not wanting to miss a second of what the dancer is telling them. A single movement can be worth many hours, even years, but you have to find the right sense for this movement. You can't lie. A lie is horrible in normal life, and even more so in dance._____**What is it, lying in dance?** At some point, you let go of everything you have accumulated, because all of it, up to the merest nuance, becomes your life and your essence. But this can only happen after an enormous amount of work. And then you won't be lying. You come on stage stripped of your name and status. You are here to show not your mastery, but your findings and realisations. _____In other words, it's letting go of the ego. Your challenge is to become as clear a channel as possible, so that you won't distort the signal that you are conveying. Exactly. As they say, dancing is praying. Once you discover that state, what other meanings can you search for in life? You are just helping others to see what you are able to see.

1

$\frac{en}{de}$ CODING

Any language is basically a code, a system of symbols that describes a certain realm, be it a nation or a branch of science. In the creative Multiverse, encoding is a method, in which one seeks to deduce such codes in order to translate (=explain) one realm into the language of another.

"If your creative language consisted of words, what would the *keywords* be ?

CARLO RATTI

(above, bottom row) 5-MINUTE SELFIE, a vertical selfie-drawing plotter, 2014

(above and facing, top row) LOCAL WARMING, an energy-savvy heating device controlled by a motion sensor
to provide the user with a personal cloud of "direct and localised warmth in an otherwise cold environment" 2013–14

CARLO RATTI

architect, engineer, inventor

A large part of your work is about decoding the language in which our environment talks to us. How do you detect the possibilities for such dialogue? Thanks to digital technologies—and in particular pervasive sensing—we can understand our cities to an unprecedented extent. What is happening at an urban scale today is similar to what happened two decades ago in Formula 1 auto racing. Up to that point, success on the circuit was primarily credited to a car's mechanics and the driver's capabilities. But then telemetry technology blossomed. The car was transformed into a computer that was monitored in real time by thousands of sensors, becoming 'intelligent' and better able to respond to the conditions of the race. _____In a similar way, over the past decade digital technologies have begun to blanket our cities, forming the backbone of a large, intelligent infrastructure. Broadband fibre-optic and wireless telecommunications grids are supporting mobile phones, smartphones and tablets that are increasingly affordable. At the same time, open databases—especially from the government—that people can read and add to are revealing all kinds of information, and public kiosks and displays are helping literate and illiterate people access it. Add to this foundation a relentlessly growing network of sensors and digital-control technologies, all tied together by cheap, powerful computers, and our cities are quickly becoming like 'computers in open air'._____How does the task of an architect—and of a creative individual in a broader sense—change in the emerging hybrid space between the digital and the physical world? This space offers a lot of possibilities for architects and designers. Architecture was always concerned with designing interfaces between people and their environment. When we lived in the cave, this environment was made of atoms; today it is a hybrid space made of bits and atoms. The definition of architecture has not changed, but architects have to face a new reality._____Another aspect is increased collaboration. The solitary, Promethean ambition of the architect has characterized most of 20th-century architecture. Today, a more collaborative approach is emerging, rooted in Internet culture and in the new paradigms of online collaboration. We explore some of these issues in our book *Open Source Architecture* proposing the emergence of a 'choral architect', who draws on participatory tools to shape design._____What will be the new forms of expression in the civilization defined by digital, bio- and nanotechnologies? We need to understand that the new forms of expression will not be only physical, but cyber-physical, as researchers

We should play @ the inter+section of *physical,* *digital* & *biological* worlds

>

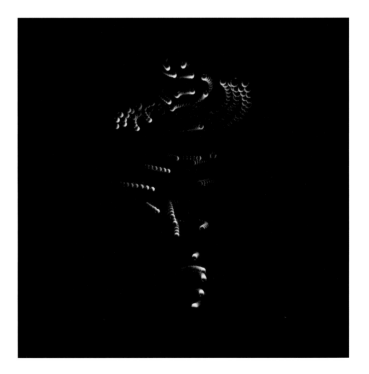

(above and facing page, top row) MAKR SHAKR, industrial robotic hand as an app-guided cocktail-mixer, 2013
(above and facing page, bottom row) DANCING ATOMS, exploring the limits of human motion with a digital pixel map of Italy's étoile dancer, Roberto Bolle, 2011

usually say. We should play at the crossroads of the physical, digital and biological worlds._____What is the place for people in the reality where a large amount of work will be performed by robots? I believe that this process in general is a positive one: what kind of life was it on a 20th-century production line, tuning one bolt after another one? I think that we should all be pleased that such work can today be outsourced to robots. People, in turn, can focus on more creative tasks, as in the old utopia of the 'Homo Ludens'(man at play) outlined in the 20th century by Dutch artist and architect Constant Nieuwenhuys._____Nieuwenhuys envisions a future where humans pursue a life of creative play, once machines take over every mundane task: "In the worldwide city of the future . . . a society of total automation, the need to work is replaced by a nomadic life of creative play, a modern return to Eden. The 'homo ludens', whom man will become once freed from labor will not have to make art, for he can be creative in the practice of his daily life."_____New ways of interaction are being developed between people and their environment (architecture, objects, etc). What expectations can this create in the artistic domain? Art is about creating new worlds starting from our everyday experience. As John Dewey wrote in *Art as Experience*: "Every work of art follows the plan of, and pattern of a complete experience, rendering it more intensely and concentratedly felt." Today, our everyday experience is undergoing an extreme transformation; this, in turn, is probably going to create change in art. But again, we need to be able to play with our hybrid world, without searching for answers in the old tools. Also, we could argue that interactions between people are becoming more complex, thanks to the Internet. If we build on Nieuwenhuys's ideas, could we say that we might become collaborative Homines Ludentes, able to invent and learn together?

(facing) The DIGITAL WATER PAVILION with a digitally operated water wall, World Expo Zaragoza, Spain, 2008

TOYO ITO

TOYO ITO
architect

Nature has a great influence on your work. How do you translate the language of nature into that of architecture? By visualising the order (spirals, spires and flowing air) in nature and transforming it into the order of architecture._____How do you combine openness to nature with the ever-growing importance of media technologies? Rather than creating *forms*, it is more important to consider architecture as a *dynamic and fluid moving body*._____How is architecture going to evolve in this age of experiments in connecting real and virtual worlds that become more and more advanced? Architecture eventually becomes an aggregate of *matter*. The role of architecture as *matter* will be more and more important . . . like the actual body of human beings._____What kind of new capabilities do you believe people need to develop or which limitations to overcome? The speed of change in the social phenomena is accelerating. However, the most important thing is to find something that is constant and to persist in it._____Which other disciplines do you believe architecture should today look at and borrow from? Rather than borrowing from the scientific concepts of the 20th century, contemporary architecture should consider human beings as a living entity as a whole, similar to the philosophy behind Eastern medicine.

Human beings

are

a **PART** of *nature*

,

architecture

is also

a **PART** of NATURE

(above, top) TAMA ART UNIVERSITY LIBRARY, Tokyo, 2007 :: (bottom) ZA KOENJI PUBLIC THEATRE, Tokyo, 2009
(facing) Construction work at the NATIONAL TAICHUNG THEATRE, Taichung, inaugurated in 2014

FRANCiS KURKDJiAN

FRANCIS KURKDJIAN

perfumer, artist

You work with olfactory sensations for which language has not even found specific words. When we speak of scents, we use metaphors, borrow words characterizing other sensations or even simply say "the scent of jasmine". And yet, at the same time, it is a skill requiring the utmost precision. A smell is connected to its olfactory memory. When I smell something, my brain does or does not recognize it. If it recognizes it, then it can give it a name; we know the smell of toast, we have learned it. If tomorrow I smell something new, I will ask myself if I know of anything comparable. In this way I come to know it by similitude, until the point when it is explained to me that it smells of a certain thing and I can then attach a name to it. And, since a sense of smell is connected to the most primitive human senses—particularly the vital sense of safety and survival—if the brain does not recognize the smell, it alerts us to danger. This is especially important when experimenting with new combinations: bringing out a particularly unusual perfume can be difficult to manage from the olfactory point of view because suddenly one feels threatened. So this is why you follow two parallel activities. The first, to create commercial perfumes, the other, free experimentation. How and why is the trade of perfumer evolving? It is evolving because technology is evolving. It's like with music: today we have sounds that didn't exist a hundred years ago and so, with new sounds, you can do new things.

(facing) An olfactory performance created for the European Night of Museums at the Grand Palais, Paris, 2011

WHAT makes a great PERFUME? — A shared collective *e—motion.*

(above, left to right) Olfactory installations involving light and music, 2007–13. CHUTT . . . D'EAU in Versailles, with metallic rose-scented fountains and light and mist effects. THE LIGHT OF THE INNOCENT, Florence. THE KING IS DANCING, Versailles. FLORA TOURNICOTA, a collaboration with Albert Schrurs of Allegory Studio

I have new raw materials that I treat differently. And then there is a movement that lays greater stress on the sense of smell. Fifty years ago, no one perfumed a hotel; perfumed candles were only just beginning whereas today they are everywhere. People are exposed more to perfumes via different mediums: household products are all perfumed; carparks are perfumed as are hotels and even restaurants. There is a return to the use of smell in society which is very important because it is a very elemental and true sense. You can't lie with scents. You can dress in a colour you don't like but with scents there is something much more visceral, intimate and physiological that, if we don't like a particular smell we feel a kind of revulsion. If I don't like this picture, I will still go on looking at it; my eyes will scan it automatically. If I don't like a smell, my nose closes to prevent me feeling sick. The degree of emotional penetration by smell is much greater than that of sound and sight. In Patrick Süskind's *Perfume*, the protagonist is able to change his identity and thus determine how he is perceived by others just by changing his smell . . . According to a study carried out at Tours University, smell can change our perception of an event. They designed a test where a panel asked a candidate questions. All candidates were asked the same questions in the same order in a room where, for one group, a scent had been introduced while, for the other, there was no smell. The first group was very successful while the second group found the interview very unsettling. A perfume can make the world seem much rosier than it is in reality._____Another thing we learn from *Perfume* is that the smell of the ingredients of a perfume may bear little resemblance to the final product. Of the raw materials used to create as end product the scent of lily-of-the-valley, not one of them on its own smells of the flower. You mix together notes of pink, green and floral white: in my bottle these three molecules exist, but when they emerge from the bottle there is a scent of lily-of-the-valley._____So it's not so much a fusion as a kind of coexistence, a type of collaboration . . . Are there certain collaborations that have opened new doors for you? The collaboration with Sophie Calle, for example, where I was asked to create my idea of the smell of money. I started out from many different things: coins that smell of metal with its rusty, metallic scent; a dollar bill with its highly individual smell of ink and paper and then also the notions of *Pecunia non olet* (money does not smell) and the laundering of dirty money . . . All this, both conceptual and physical, became a smell, but not strictly speaking the smell of money because, in the end, I started from my memories. I collaborated with Hratch Arbach, a Syrian artist of Armenian origin based in New York. This was *Mawtini* ('our land' in Arabic), an installation made in the church of Saint-Séverin based on the idea that artists are on earth to absorb the pain of the world, digest it and bring beauty from it. Arbach made thousands of crucifixion nails out of wax that I perfumed with three different scents: blood, earth and jasmine. Visitors were invited to take the nails and, at the end of the visit, place them on an altar consisting of a heated plate. The nails melted on the hot metal, the art installation being the release of the blended smells. The collective gesture of people laying down their pain and sorrow became itself the artistic work._____How do you move from an idea to a scent? How does the 'translation' come about? Through feelings. I have my idea; this idea creates an emotion. My creative process is that my perfume must give me the same emotion that I received from my idea. It's simple._____In this it chimes with dance where one does not 'understand', one 'feels'. It's like that with perfume. A great perfume is a shared collective emotion. It's like the fascination of a work of art experienced by everyone at once, making this work popular; we recognize ourselves collectively in this artistic production. The thing that makes a great perfume is that, even if people do not understand the point of departure, they will understand the point of arrival. I stop working when the emotion in the bottle corresponds to the feelings I had at the beginning before I had even begun to create the scent._____What is the keyword in your work? Emotion.

MAWTINI, a collaboration with the artist Hratch Arbach. Saint-Séverin church, Paris, 2014

PHILIPPE RAHM

(below) EVAPORATED ROOMS, the interior and the thermal diagram of the apartment designed for Louis Malachane, a medical doctor based in Lyon, 2012 :: (facing) A demo version of meteorological architecture in the DOMESTIC ASTRONOMY installation designed for the Louisiana Museum of Modern Art (Denmark), 2009. The heat generated by electric light bulbs is normally a waste by-product, but in this project it is used to create a microclimate that determines the placement of the apartment's cooler or warmer rooms

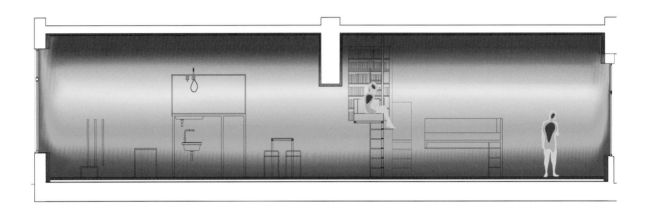

PHILIPPE RAHM

architect

A rather conventional architectural practice at the beginning, in the 2000s we started investigating the invisible parameters that define a space: light, the chemical quality of air, electromagnetic waves and their relation to our physiology. The work I did between 2000 and 2005 was a way of redefining the language of architecture. When I represented Switzerland at the Venice Biennale, we created the *Hormonorium,* an all-white space in which the floor emitted extremely bright light that blocked the production of the 'sleep hormone' melatonin, making the visitors feel more active and alert. We also adjusted the oxygen levels to imitate the high-altitude atmosphere. This affected the level of the EPO hormone, which stimulates the production of blood cells that bring more oxygen inside your muscles, so that you feel stronger. People could experience that space not only through their five senses but also through the hormonal cycles of their bodies. We wanted to show that architecture is a field where you can start with physiology and go towards meteorology._____What are the reasons behind your interest in this particular research? And what are the keywords of your design language? Architecture is about the space and the invisible. As you enter a building, you get immersed in the air, the light, the particles . . . Of course, to design a space, you have to design its envelope; architects design forms in order to create a pocket of air where the climate is different from the climate outside. I wished to go back to the original mission of architecture, which is to protect the inner space from the rain; to keep it warm when it's cold outside. As an architect, you build voids, not solids. And if you need to build a void, you have to work with its materiality, which is the invisible things such as air and light. You build an atmosphere; you design a climate. How do you design a void? In Switzerland, in order to reduce energy consumption, it is recommended to heat different rooms at different temperatures. In the bedroom, heating can be reduced because we stay under the blanket; the living room should be warmer because here we mostly sit on a sofa, while the bathroom, where we are naked and wet, should be even warmer. If you want to do this [in a traditional way], you need rooms with the doors that should always stay closed in order to isolate the differently heated spaces, but this sounds so 19th century! What we propose instead is the design that follows the temperature. For example, the air is always colder close to the floor and warmer towards the ceiling. Normally, we heat the lower part of the room, but no one uses the warm space under the ceiling, so we simply lose a lot of energy. We suggest using this space—for instance, by raising the bathtub towards the ceiling since the bathroom should be the warmest place in the whole apartment._____In other words, you follow the natural air flow to create an open space in which the bedroom,

Architecture as

— > constructed atmosphere

DIURNISM at the Centre Pompidou, Paris, 2007. To create 'night during the day', the space is filled with orange-yellow light, which prompts the human organism to produce the same amount of the 'sleep hormone' melatonin as it does at night

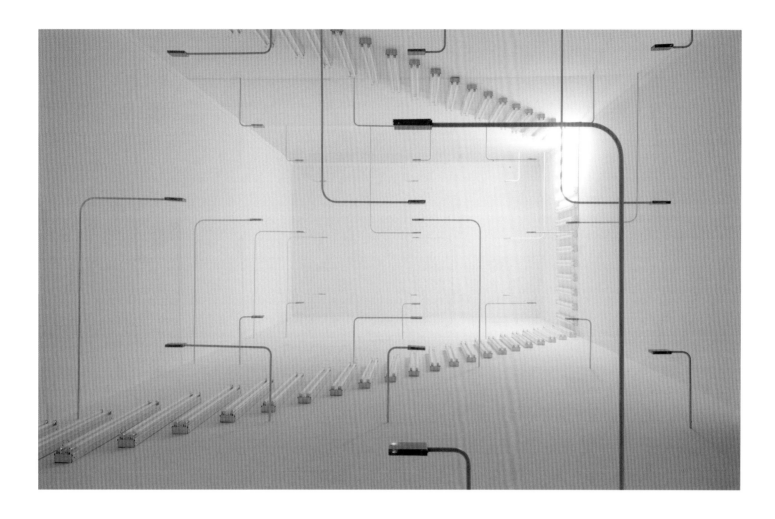

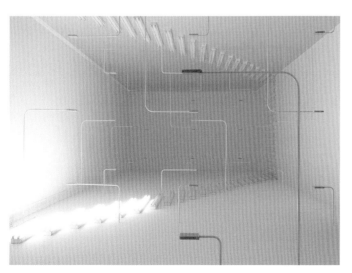
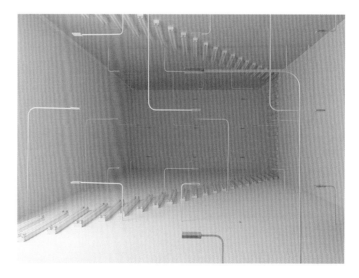

INTERIOR WEATHER at the Canadian Centre for Architecture, Montréal, 2007. As the moving light source echoes the earth's movement around the sun, it modifies the climatic parametres of the room and creates a 'constantly evolving three-dimensional geography' with its warmer or cooler, drier or more damp areas

the bathroom, the kitchen are all placed at different heights. In this way, you use the entire volume available of an apartment and transform a familiar setting into a new kind of topography shaped by invisible natural phenomena. The idea is that, if we design the climate first, the form of the space comes as a consequence. You reinvent the way you design and use the space._____And the materials you work with are, basically, air and light. Normally, in architecture you have elements like stairs, columns or walls. The subjects of our architecture are air, light, heat, humidity. If you work with solid elements, you organise masses, use addition, symmetry, include one thing inside another. In our case, architectural composition uses not geometric, but meteorological tools such as convection, evaporation, conduction, radiation. We analyse different parameters of the climate and different physical processes to see how we can reengage form and function according to these._____What about light? In your designs, light should obviously do more than simply illuminate a room. The starting point of our project called *Diurnism* is that modernity creates the endless day in the city. By controlling the wavelengths of the electric lighting, we created the night inside this endless day. In another project, the *Split Times Café*, we show that architecture can be used to build not only the space, but also the time. Glass walls with different colour filters create different ambiences that guide the visitors' behaviour, from the blue filter in the area for dynamic short meetings to the yellow filter for a lounging mood. It's like building day and night. Why have you changed the definition of your architecture from 'physiological' to 'meteorological'? 'Physiological' refers to the way in which this architecture relates to the body, while 'meteorological' is a tool for designing spaces. So, it was not about changing; it was about expanding the field of research.

58

(facing) HORMONORIUM, a collaboration with Jean-Gilles Décosterd, presented at the 8. Architecture Biennale of Venice, 2002

2

CONCENTRATION

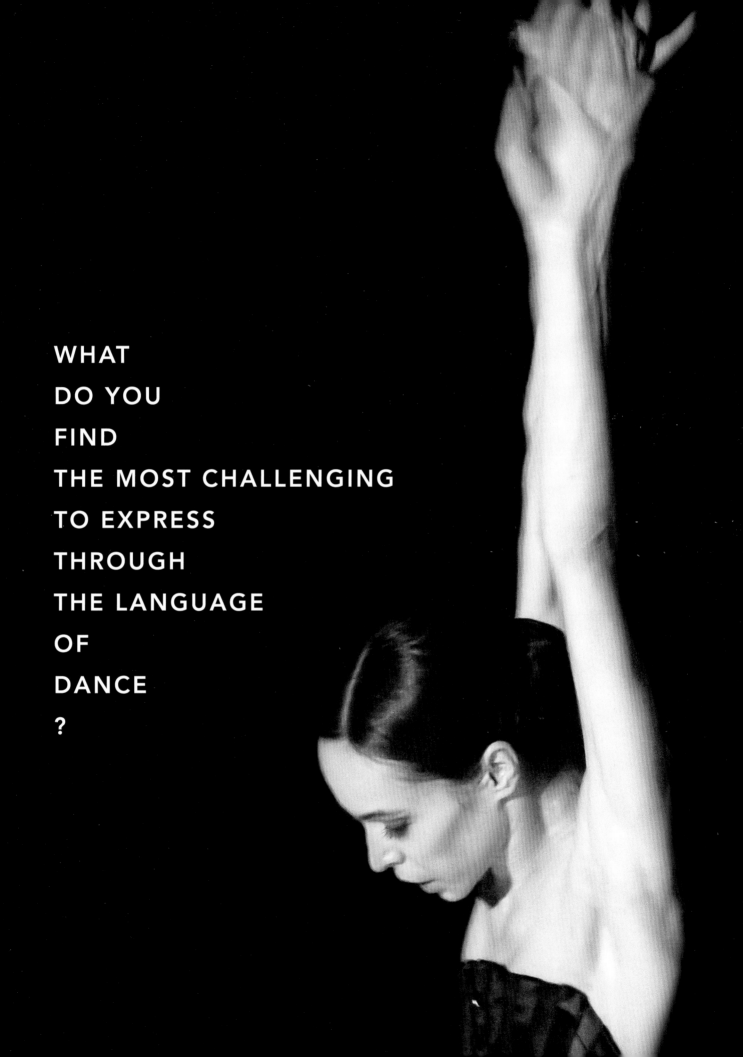

WHAT
DO YOU
FIND
THE MOST CHALLENGING
TO EXPRESS
THROUGH
THE LANGUAGE
OF
DANCE
?

ANGELIN PRELJOCAJ

ANGELIN PRELJOCAJ

contemporary dance choreographer

We often think of dance as an expression of the body but in reality it is the relationship between body and space. More mysterious still is another dance—one that is the constantly changing space between the bodies of the dancers. A pas de deux, for example, can be seen as the modulation of space between two dancers. If the space decreases slowly, it may be an expression of love, if suddenly, a mood of violence—and yet it consists of nothing more than the way in which this space opens and closes!_____I remember my art teacher telling us not to draw the objects but the spaces between them. That's exactly what has been going on in the thirty years I have been a choreographer! You could say that I spend every day refining space. Naturally, I then go on to work with the dancers on movement, quality, precision, dynamics, but I am thinking all the time about space. Sometimes I think my work consists of making time apparent and space visible; of creating time and space._____Just as in your artistic work, the question "What can the body do?" is fundamental to Spinoza's philosophy. He also spoke about active and passive emotions, meaning those that are conscious and those that are unconscious. Is it important for you that your audience is aware of its feelings? I strongly believe that, as Marcel Duchamp put it, it is the viewer that makes the work. The artist offers us an object—in the broadest sense of the word—onto which the viewer can project his or her own ideas. The important thing today is not to create something beautiful and polished; the purpose is in the doing. I believe that, in the Louvre at nighttime, the Mona Lisa doesn't

Angelin Preljocaj's interview is illustrated with photographs of the ballet Le Parc

exist at all; it does not become real until the first visitor comes and looks at it. A work of art only exists if it is activated by someone, just as, according to some scientists, the universe only exists because we are thinking about it._____It's quite disturbing when you realize that we only see the past. Everything we see has already happened; there is no moment when we see the present._____But at the same time, the present is the key notion in dance which only exists in the present. All these ideas fascinate me because they lead to a constant reappraisal of my work. I like experimenting with pure movement. At these times, my chief preoccupations are with weight, energy, time and space—something akin to physics or mathematics. I like it that these experiments can then go on to be used in a narrative and perhaps reconnect with ballet's great classics such as *Swan Lake*.

...my work consists of making *time*_____apparent & **space**_____visible.

In more radical works like *Empty Moves*, which is really a study in pure movement, I think I have almost succeeded in achieving total abstraction. This ballet was inspired by a John Cage piece called *Empty Words*, a deconstruction of a text by Henry David Thoreau rearranged and disarranged by Cage to give a kind of entirely abstract poetry. I need this kind of permanent laboratory for research into movement so that I can go on to create more narrative ballets, because I like telling stories. But just because I'm going to tell the story of Snow White, it doesn't mean that I'll abandon the texture of my choreographical work. No matter what extract you choose from *Blanche Neige*, *Roméo et Juliette* or *Le Parc*, it is essentially all about weight, energy, space and time. And, at the same time, you're having to deal with the body because a body has physical limitations and limitations—even if we try every day to overcome them—in technique, plasticity and distortion._____**There was another aspect that you referred to: the fact that dancers' bodies are formed by their origins, by the cultures they come from.** I'm often told that my ballets are abstract. That's true, but, in fact, dance is never totally abstract because each body comes with its own history. When a dancer enters the studio, it is possible to interpret many things about his body, and my work as a choreographer begins from that point. In my view there is nothing more concrete than the body which is why—even in the most abstract of works—dance remains a step away from abstraction. Anyone entering the stage has their own story and, when they start to move, it is that story that is set in motion and becomes reality._____Choreography is an extremely complex and endless area of research. For me, dance is at the very beginning of its history. Painting and the first cave drawings happened thousands of years ago but the history of dance as something performed on a stage is very recent, only a few hundred years old.

JOHN NEUMEIER

Tatiana (2014)

JOHN NEUMEIER

choreographer, director

As someone reputed for being able to choreograph virtually any human state, what do you find the most challenging to express through dance? We can start with what is impossible. Specific information, the kind you can read in a newspaper, cannot be expressed. Quoting Balanchine, it's impossible to say 'mother-in-law' in ballet._____**Probably you don't even need to.** Because it's not important. Our mission is not to communicate information but to invent reality in the present tense and present it on stage. It needs an observer who puts himself into what he sees in order to feel it. I don't say 'understand it', because understanding is not important. Feeling is important. It's like in a dream. Our dreams do not have a logic, but they have a reality for us, which is very profound. We are deeply afraid, deeply in love, deeply ecstatic, and it is a reality, but it is not something we understand in terms of 'why' or 'where'. I can only work from my intuition about what I can express at this particular moment. But even saying this makes it sound wrong, because what I do is not the result of some rational analysis. If I prepare the ballet *Tatiana*, I study the text, I have my own thoughts about it, I read what Nabokov and other people thought about it, but when I start to create, I forget all of this and try to concentrate on the present moment, acting spontaneously. I begin to simply move without thinking or asking questions. Questioning what is difficult may only occur in the beginning or in the end, when I look at what I have done and use my head to judge and criticise. But the most important is what I don't think about._____**Michelangelo used to say that he only had to remove the excess marble and set free the figure contained inside. You should probably relate to this description of the creative process.** I always use this example when I do

___Even if I am creating **a world** that I don't completely understand in order to get cl**O**ser to it,' I have to go from a part of this world _that I find in my heart_

symphonic work. For me, music is like that stone. I have to wait and find what is it in the stone that I can discover. Maybe you can take the same stone and find a different way. This has very much to do with my creative process. First, I ask my-self: can you do *St Matthew Passion* as a ballet? For years, I didn't know, but one day it came to me. I could see the top of this mountain. I didn't know which way to go, but I agreed to take the first step, because with this first step I could realise whether I would fall down or find one stone after another [to reach the summit]. You rely on intuition and spontaneity, yet at the same time have a profound need to study the subject in a very scholarly way. At which point do these two approaches come together? You create only from what you are, but you can en-rich yourself. If you eat the right food, it becomes part of you._____It forms that block of stone with which you will later work? That's right. But, as you be-gin to work, you must have the courage to forget all of this. It shouldn't be like, I go to the studio and look up what I have written in my notebook, because I thought it was very beautiful the moment I sketched it. I must be free from that which I thought was important. Sometimes, halfway up the mountain, I may need some

(below and facing) <u>Dialogue</u>, *a ballet created for Diana Vishneva, 2007*

intellectual refreshment to continue my way, but still I will not use that as a reference. There is in me a love of knowledge and an appreciation of the great things other people have done—the pictures, sculptures, music that I can make a part of myself. Not to copy, but to let it be a part of me, and, when this happens, this 'me' can make something new._____How does one make a creation alive? This is something we must not ask! I do believe that creation is a mystery. It's based on love. You can be in love with the act of creation, and this is the greatest motivation. For me, the journey of creation is more important than the destination. When I see the result, I'm always critical, and always changing. For me, the greatest joy would be to create a work that would never have a premiere, that would always be in the state of development, so that I could always come in, and look, and say: "I would like to add another character, and change the lighting, and I think the costume should be green rather than red." I don't want to watch what I did and say: "Oh, it's so beautiful!" We are always looking for perfection, but I have never attained it in my work. It sometimes happens that I can find no other answer, so I have to leave it as it is, but that doesn't mean it's perfect._____To me, the idea of a continuous process of creation that doesn't require any final result curiously resonates with the quantum theory—in the sense that all potentials exist simultaneously until the observer appears, and it's only the observer's presence that turns it into an either/or situation. Exactly. But in a ballet, I tell my dancers that there is only one performance: this one. Not "I am doing Giselle," but "I am doing *this* Giselle." And then the spectator comes and says: "This is what I saw," except that every spectator saw something different. When I am in Hamburg, I watch every performance by my company, because I keep thinking what else I can do; how I can rearrange the given things that are already there, and what it will mean. We are very fortunate, because our art is the art completely of the present tense. Whether it is *Sleeping Beauty*, the Noh theatre or modern choreography, when the curtain opens, it is always *now*. One can learn the forms of the past, but the content must be 'now'.

(facing) Lady of the Camelias, 2011 :: (following pages) Tatiana, 2014

78

3

X $\frac{te}{pa}$ NSION

– is about adding new capabilities that take you outside the standard range; becoming bigger. «To extend» also means to hold (something) out towards someone.

"What kind of [EXTRA]capabilities do we need ?

Which human limit[ation]s do you seek to *overcome* through your work ?

ROSS LOVE GROVE

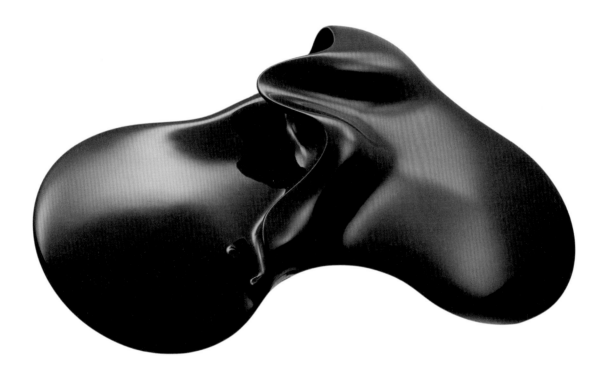

(above) RIDON, carbon fibre motorcycle, 2009 :: (facing) VOID ILLUSION, carbon fibre table and suspended light, 2012

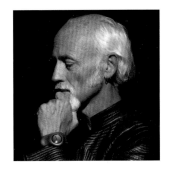

ROSS LOVEGROVE

industrial designer

When I went to the Royal College of Art in the 1980s, they'd never find me in my department. I would be everywhere—in fashion, in textiles . . . When I was in Manchester doing my first degree, there was a ballet school next door, and I spent every lunchtime there because I loved the way those people moved. I like the idea of blending, transferring and converging different realms of creativity. When you think like an artist, you break boundaries very naturally. What man thinks often becomes reality; it's only a matter of time. Cars will fly because it has been set in our minds since Fritz Lang's movies. The world is changing in its mindsets, technology, performance levels, and I want to work at the cutting edge of the time in which we live. I work as a sculptor of technology; I am the portal of how a headphone in your ear might feel, or wrapping an aircraft seat around you so that you feel cocooned and protected._____When our ancestors lived in caves they developed a heightened sense of awareness to survive, there was this incredible moment in our evolution where our senses were very alive, and the way we interacted with space was different. We haven't lost these primordial instinctive feelings; beneath the high tech urban society and the digital age we are immersing ourselves in, I am looking to touch people deeply with the objects I create._____**How do you decide when a project is complete?** I work in two polarities. One is pure self-expression, like my *Cellular Automata* series which are scans through the spine of a living human

I work as a SCULPTOR of _tech_nology :: I _wrap_ <u>TECHNOLOGY</u> <u>around</u> _**humans**_

being, magnified and 3D printed. These resonate with humanity because the source comes from within us; when I manipulate them, I can play like a divine entity changing an evolutionary code. I can't do that as a designer. Similarly, in 2001 I designed the _Ty Nant_ water bottle, one of the first digitally generated products of all times. It captured the essence of natural forces so that the economics of nature became animated in your hand. I convinced a medical technician who undertook facial scanning and rebuilding out of his laboratory and got him to work for me, because I needed a new process to advance the sculpting of materials via technology. When the first bottle arrived, I thought I had failed. But then I put water in it, and the 'skin' disappeared. It was like discovering an icon of water itself as form moves people silently, without language. _Ridon_, which is an anagram of Rodin, looks like a motorbike, but it's not. These are my studies into where man and machine converge. **What extra capabilities do you believe people need?** I'm thinking of Hugh Herr, the rock climber, biophysicist and bionic limbs engineer, who lost both

MOOT (Mood Of Our Time), carbon fibre chair, 2013

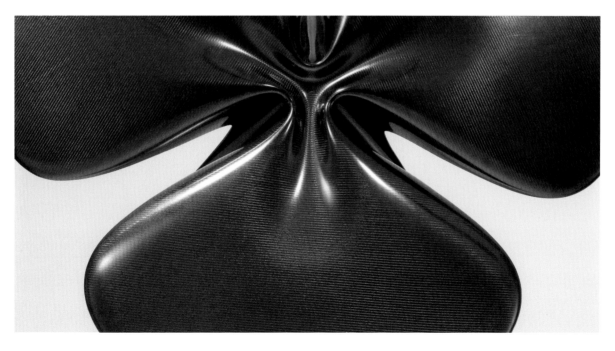

(above) GINGKO, carbon fibre table, 2007 :: (page 93) ILABO, gravitational 3D printed shoes for United Nude, 2015

legs at the age of seventeen and designed the prostheses that outperformed the 'regular' limbs. Often the driver for innovation is a situation where somebody is so determined to overcome an impediment. From a design perspective, what can studying the biomechanics exoskeletons lead to? Putting something outside the body, as in the case of a turtle shell, is an evolutionary innovation and natural adaptation. Beauty and logic meet where hard and soft elements converge so that balance, harmony and physiognomy coalesce biologically. With body scanning and 3D printing technologies, you can create forms that feel like they have been grown specifically for you. Take the *Ilabo* shoe, which has started with human hair as a reference and looks as though it flows around your foot. Actor Willem Dafoe said: "In film, you capture. In theatre, you conjure." Do you capture or do you conjure? In film, you can convey a higher level of augmented reality, but I am interested in the authentic, the tactile, the closeness, the breath. This is why I think that the stage is still a great place . . . maybe with a degree of hybridisation with other techniques, because today we are trained to multi-task. We deal with so much information that when we are shown something that is over-simplified, we see that either as relaxation for the mind, or as dumbing down; but I fully believe that people have an amazing ability to absorb complexity, and that the capacity of the brain has evolved to understand our place in the universe. How does one project complexity? I am working with a company called Emotiv Insight who have developed a device where a child can visualise an object and it can be 3D printed from his neural transmission. When they asked why I was particularly interested in it, I replied that I'd like to be able to imagine something and have it 3D printed directly from my imagination. Indeed, what frustrates me is the idea of having to press a square key on a keyboard to make organic design. To me, it's a limitation, and it's unnatural. A dancer can explore a new movement in front of a mirror; I want to be able to create as directly as I am talking to you.

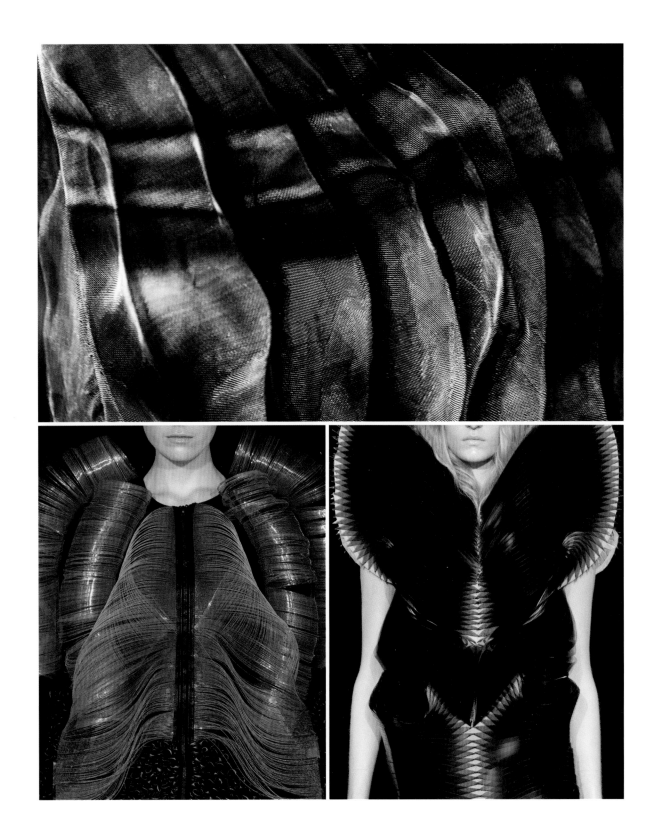

(top) detail of a garment made from ultra-thin metal mesh coloured by burning and pleated, HACKING INFINITY collection, 2015
(bottom) garments from the collections CRYSTALLISATION (left), 2010, and ESCAPISM (right), 2011

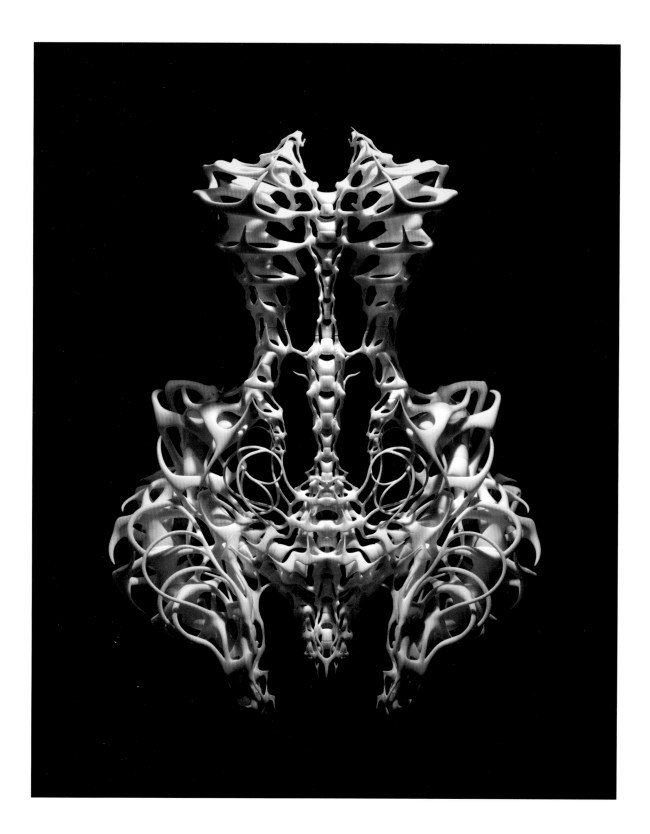

(above) a 3D-printed dress from the ESCAPISM collection, 2011

IRIS VAN HERPEN

fashion designer

Why have you chosen garment design as your artistic medium? When I was younger, I planned to become a classical dancer, but then I started collecting materials and sculpting. I always loved creating something with my hands. When I work on a garment, I use the body as my base and my inspiration source; this is something I took from my dance background. It's my way of combining dance, which is an abstract means of expression, with materiality, and I can use my hands to create sculptures for the body, so this is where everything comes together for me. And I also have my 'trips' outside fashion, my collaborations. I would be scared to devote my entire life to just one thing without trying to expand beyond that._____**What do your designs do for the body?** I don't believe that a person has only one identity; we all have different layers of who we are. The body itself and its movements give me enough information to work with, while identities can change. Wearing a garment can bring into you some different kind of energy; that's what I hope my garments do._____**Collaborative projects, joining forces with other creators seems to be an integral part of your design approach.** It's always a dialogue. Giving someone a drawing and telling them "I need this" is not collaboration; it's outsourcing. The people I work with contribute something bigger than just their skills. It's about talking to each other, discussing new concepts and finding mutual excitement that gives you enough energy to go through difficult periods when you need to bring together and balance your ideas. One of my most important collaborators is the architect Philip Beesley. He is a huge expert in technology, systems and machinery, and at the same time he sees the world like a work of art. He can be very technical and very poetic, all at once. Together, we work on structures. This may sound too intellectual, but the essence of our cooperation is really intuitive and primitive. We start with small hand-made samples followed by a long development process, but the beginning is always very playful._____Collaborations are the core of my inspiration and my driving force, too. I am driven not by the collections, but by the ideas that can't be realised just yet. If I continue working on them, some of it will become possible in five or ten years, while seasonal collections are about capturing the moment where I am now. Deadlines require me to make decisions, otherwise I would have lost myself in experimentation. On the other hand, I need collaborations because they give me something in the long run._____**What is your relationship with science and technology?** Science has a big influence on our world view. It explores the matters we don't see and don't understand, and I am always fascinated by such things. CERN *[the European Organisation for Nuclear Research]*, with its huge underground machines

It's *beautiful* __WHEN__ people develop a LANGUAGE *together*

(above) the magnetic grown dress from the WILDERNESS EMBODIED collection was created in collaboration with Jolan van der Wiel, 2014
(facing) the WATER DRESS from the CRYSTALLISATION collection, 2010

that look like sculptures, is one of the most beautiful places I have ever been to. It was a mind-blowing experience as most of the things they do are beyond even my imagination! *Magnetic Motion* was inspired by my first visit there *[the Arts@CERN team cites the CMS detector with a magnetic field that is 100,000 times stronger than the Earth's as a source of inspiration for this collection]*. Most of all, it was the conversations with the CERN scientists, the free thinkers, that gave me the energy to work on this collection, to expand my imagination. Together with the artist Jolan van der Wiel we experimented in growing structures with the help of magnets *[These experimental pieces use a material that contains a mix of iron filings and resin and is manipulated with magnets to form irregular spiky textures]*. Drawing inspiration from natural processes and combining this with new technologies is essential to my work. Experiments with magnetism produced a beautiful contrast between controlling the process up to a certain point and then surrendering control to the natural forces. We had to mix the ingredients with laboratory-like precision, but the process itself took just a few seconds, and the design was done!_____In the *BioPiracy* collection, did you really shrink-wrap the models in those plastic bags? It was not a bag but two separate plastic sheets, with two tubes to maintain the air circulation. It's an installation by Lawrence Malstaf whose works focus on meditative states. Before proposing this to the models, I tested it myself. I did not expect it to be such a pleasant experience. You felt supported and protected; you could stay there forever. Malstaf compares it to being inside a womb. Placed in that vacuum, you no longer sense the space around you. You hear nothing except your own breath. You are really connected to your body, because that's where all your attention is. One of the models called me the next day to say that she missed hanging inside the bag!

(facing) SHRINK, the installation by Lawrence Malstaf as part of van Herpen's BIOPIRACY fashion show, 2014

ENKI
BiLAL

ENKI BILAL

artist, filmmaker

By their nature, comics are a synthetic art that combines drawing and literature with choreographic, cinematic and architectural mentality . . . That's an unconventional definition; they usually say that comics were intended for those who can't read and therefore prefer to look at pictures. But comics are indeed an extremely hybrid genre. I have first discovered them when I was a boy in Belgrade. When I came to live in France at the age of ten, not only did I fall in love with the French language, but also realised that there existed a big tradition of Franco-Belgian comics. I could thus unite my passions: drawing and the new language, but only much later I was able to appreciate how powerful those tools could be. Add body and movement, and you end up with a kind of choreography, while architecture helps in constructing the story, in which the ellipses are not the same as in literature or film. Eventually you master the language and start emancipating it. My work today has little to do with traditional comic books. Experimenting in various domains, from cinema to choreography, helps me to continuously add something new to my 'art of origin'._____Is it a natural process or a conscious effort of pushing yourself out of your comfort zone? Both. You have to find comfort in risk-taking. If you know in advance that you can do something and it will be a success, then it's a zero-risk affair; comfort degenerating into boredom. This has happened to me at a certain point; what saved me was a complete change of work style.

Your cities are never streamlined and sleek. It's an assembly of things that are conspicuously grafted onto other things, like the industrial chimneys on a baroque palace in the film *Bunker Palace Hotel*, or the Bauhaus-style cubicles in a 'post-imperial' interior in *Tykho Moon*. How do you construct the material environment of your worlds?

Reorganising chaos is my way of telling stories. I assemble these worlds out of seemingly dissociated blocks that come from different realms to be digested in the same stomach. The worlds I create speak volumes about the world I have known myself; they are shaped by the political and ideological issues of the 20th century, by Yugoslavia and other East European countries. It's a sort of mental equipment that you possess because you have been there, and, when you are free to construct a world from scratch, you surround yourself with familiar things. In this hardware shop imagination comes along with memories to create a somewhat anachronistic flavour, like placing a bakelite phone receiver in 2030—which may sound like nonsense, but I do it intentionally in order to heighten the impact. Familiar yet forgotten objects reappear as a kind of affirmation, because with a bakelite receiver everyone knows exactly what it is, while the thin bar of a contemporary mobile phone looks like a lot of things; it can be a voice recorder, a camera, a diabetes testing device . . . The worlds I describe in my stories come alive

re/organising *chaos*

with the help of this 'visual grammar', and, when we are shooting a film, I'm sometimes astonished to see how perfectly my collaborators' interpretations fit into these worlds.

A lot of your stories question the limits of our personal integrity, the extent to which

(above, top and bottom) THE DORMANT BEAST, fragments from the graphic novel, 2006 :: (facing) MECANHUMANIMAL, 2013
(page 111) ENKIBILALDEUXMILLEUN, exhibition poster, 2001

humans can be hackable. Nikopol, the character who is forced to share both his body and his mind with an Ancient Egyptian god in the *Immortal*, is one of the most dramatic examples. All my stories are about the individuals that are manipulated by the society they have created. Their only desire is to be able to define their own destiny, yet there is always something that interferes, be it a totalitarian regime or an Egyptian god. The human being is never at peace, and it is this restlessness that I put in the limelight and at times exaggerate, notably in the case of Nikopol with its incongruence between the seriousness of the problem and the eccentric manner in which it is treated. It's probably the hybrid nature of comics that gives them a strong immersive aspect. I find this quality crucial to new, evolving art forms that reboot our 'operating system' as they question our perception of reality. Our brain adapts to the radically changing world; over-communication, high-speed connection, the possibility to send messages and images in real time are seductive and addictive. The world as the older generations knew it is falling apart; their knowledge is no longer of interest to the new generations whose reasoning is different. Old references are no longer appreciated as the new culture creates its own references. Behaviours are changing, and it's only the children of this intermediate generation—the one that has perfectly mastered new technologies and facilitated telecommunications, but lost the ability to connect with others—that will be able to do both. They will be consuming more culture, but this culture they themselves are going to create. We live in a pivotal period; the mutation process starts to take shape._____In which direction do you see the new art moving? Looking from my perspective, I would say that video art is an art of the future. The evolving art of the moving image; holograms, flexible and floating screens, lots of new possibilities. In terms of sound, we are already close to perfection . . . What are they going to produce with all these tools, I don't know, but facing this great unknown is an interesting place to be.

111

CARSTEN NICOLAI

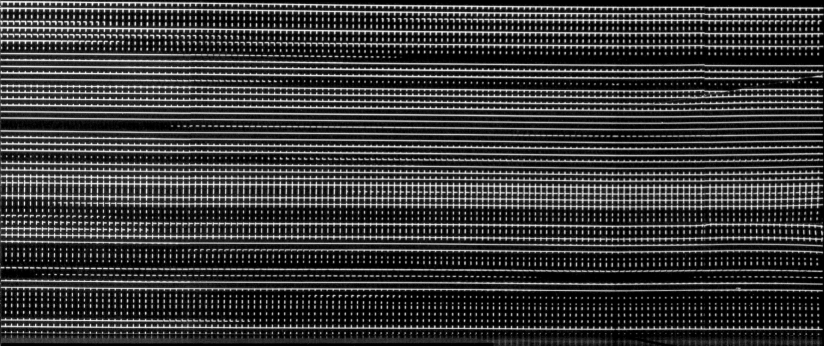

CARSTEN NICOLAI

artist, musician (Alva Noto)

In your installations, the image is used to visualise the otherwise invisible phenomena, so, in this sense, it is never 'created' by the artist. Never; that's the idea. One of the concepts that emerged from my performance work is translating sound into image. I design graphic parameters based on the sound. Take the oscilloscope; in a way, it represents the wave form of the sound—and, if you look at a wave from above, the pattern becomes a repeating black-to-white gradient . . . I am interested in the interaction between image and sound, and also in human perception. Not everything we see exists the way we see it. Our brain has a certain way of processing images. For instance, if we see something blurry, we always need to recognise a certain pattern; looking at clouds, we try to interpret them as animals. There are things we want to see and those we filter. Sometimes we cease to distinguish between dream and reality; our brain can create images that are as powerful as reality. I explore the limits of our perception and produce works that help us realise how manipulative our brain is. In one of my projects, called *uni(psycho) acoustic*, people hear a small noise but do not recognise it. Then they learn that it was a fingernail scratching the chalkboard, and this specific information makes them hear the same sound differently; it starts to cause fear. The fact that hearing is not entirely about ears, but also participates in connecting things visually, is extremely interesting, too. As

(previous pages) UNIDISPLAY, a mega-projection challenging the viewers' perception through a sequence of different visual effects, 2012

you listen to someone while looking at their mouth, you may hear different words than if you listen without seeing the moving lips. Even more surprisingly, listening to a piece in which a constant tone is interrupted by short fragments of white noise, one would hear a continuous sound because the brain adds the missing parts. Similarly, if there is a horse walking in a forest, what you actually see because of the trees are only fragments of its body, but our brain makes it whole. This, in fact, is a very 'animal' capacity that was necessary for our survival as it allowed recognising the predators._____We only perceive the tiny portion of reality that is necessary for us to function properly. It's not easy to realise how profoundly we are conditioned by our sensory capacities, and you are trying to make us aware of this. I use visualisation to bridge different kinds of perception. There are sounds that our ears can't hear, but we can make them visible. I have works based on magnetism, which is another phenomenon we can't sense. I am interested in expanding our sensory opportunities. Electromagnetic frequencies can appear as audible sounds or as visible light. They have an incredible amount of possibilities to manifest themselves. All of this is strongly connected, but our sensory organs

A lot of my ideas are about EXPANDING our PERCEPTION

(eyes, ears, etc.) separate the incoming information, and yet in the end it all comes together again._____Imagine having a skin that can see, hear and feel! Other species have this kind of sensitivity. I have read a children's book about a boy who had shrunk in order to travel with the ants. He was surprised to have ears on his legs, and

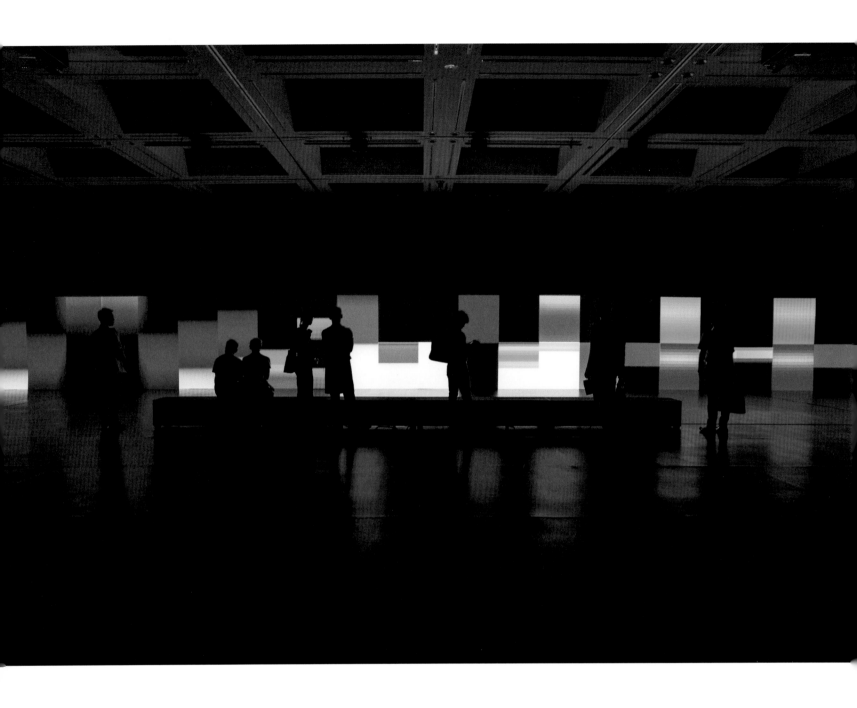

(above) UNICOLOR, an installation based on the colour theories of various scientists and artists and exploring the psychology of colour perception, 2014
(facing, top left) UNIDISPLAY, a real-time mega-projection challenging the viewers' perception through a sequence of different visual effects, 2012
(facing, bottom and top right) CRT MGN, the image of four neon tubes transmitted on a TV screen and distorted by a magnet pendulum, 2013

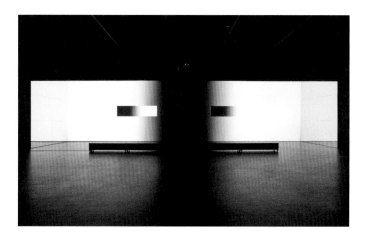
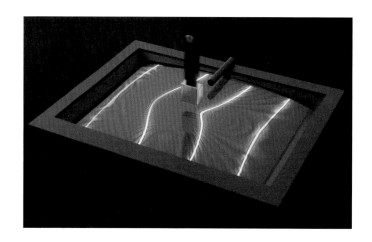
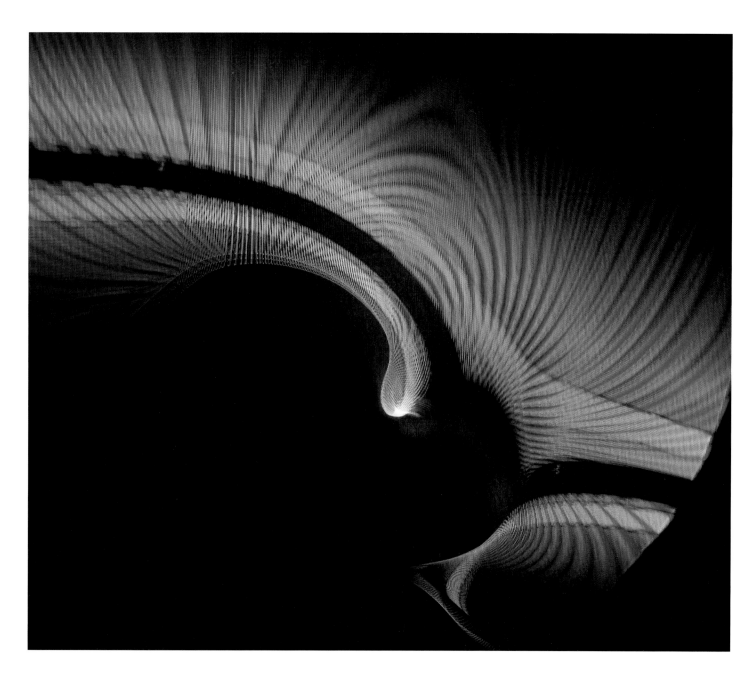

no longer on his head. We humans tend to take the way we are as common ground for all living beings, but won't a change of perspective be great? I would love to have an experience of seeing the world the way a fly does. I want to break the hierarchies of higher and lower species. I hate hierarchies; they are boxes that limit us in many ways. In your art that largely deals with 'intangibles', an error can be the only way for these intangibles to manifest themselves. For me, understanding an error is the most creative moment. We define an error as a failure, but it is the errors that make us human. Perhaps the error is the only reason why we can say that we are intelligent. An error breaks the continuity of a planned process; it is these unexpected moments that make us react. Breaking the routine is the most important thing. The routine is the most difficult part of human relations, but it's also very interesting. Machines are much better in performing routine operations, yet we praise ourselves if we can develop routines and execute them well. The polarity of wanting to become a machine but at the same time hating the idea is permanently present in us._____Machines are infinitely more performant than humans, but they can't be creative. They can, and this is exactly what I am trying to work with. They become creative the moment they malfunction. When I feed a TV with an audio instead of a video signal, as in the *telefunken* project, the TV becomes creative because it has to make something out of that signal but can't read it properly, so it starts destroying it or reacting to it. A lot of my works come from forcing specific programs to do things they are not made for. And, the moment before they completely shut down, they do things one would never expect. In my studio, I am known for opening up a brand new machine and immediately destroying it because I'd push some wrong button on purpose. Sometimes it's the only way to discover new things.

(facing, top) UNITXT, visuals based on the real-time manipulation of soft- and hardware-generated patterns by an audio signal, 2008
(bottom) TRACES, a series of photos documenting the numerous traces of cosmic and terrestrial radiation, 2007

4

SHIFT

HOW PRECISELY CAN YOUR VISION BE TRANSLATED
INTO THE FORMS INHERENT TO YOUR ART?
TO WHAT EXTENT DO YOU EXPECT THIS TRANSLATION
TO BE UNDERSTOOD BY THE VIEWER?

MARCO GOECKE

MARCO GOECKE

contemporary dance choreographer

You describe yourself as a peaceful, flexible person, and yet your choreography is extremely sharp and full of tension. Of course it's deliberate, and it also has a strong decorative aspect. There has to be a frame and a shape, but, curiously, the dancers who have worked with me say that they have always felt unbelievably free, never caged by what I proposed them, but always able to be themselves—in spite of the form being so strict and every gesture so deliberate. There is no improvisation, no emotional kitsch; it's an abstract thing that allows for emotions because it has a form._____**Maybe the reason why it feels so liberating is that you manage to uncover some instinctive, ingrained movements that are triggered by certain states or feelings? Which means that they are deliberate in a ritualistic rather than artificial way . . . Knowing that dance cannot be understood, but only experienced, what is it that you are trying to convey to your audience?** I think that the theatre today should be emptied of pictures, because we are fed up with imagery in our media-dominated world. In this respect, I am a minimalist for sure. I need to keep things simple in order to circle around a certain feeling—mine, and that of the dancers, and the feeling that is maybe shared by all of us. I have no idea what I want to express; it can be my fears, or maybe the fears of the others. In my work, fear is a very powerful element. It is my biggest resource that allows me—and, hopefully, the others, too—to set free from those fears._____**I'd also suggest that you seek to recreate the atmosphere of the dreams. Not some particular dream, but rather the awareness of being inside a dream.** Dreams are a big source, although it is never a direct translation. Around me, there is a cloud filled with beliefs, worries and fears, but also with lots

I WANTED TO LEAVE OUT  *every thing*

i knew from *other* choreographers

of humour, and that whole mix shapes my work. It's never sentimental, or melancholic, but more on the rough side._____I am trying to guess what your other inspiration sources might be. What comes to mind are cartoons and silent movies, for the intensity and sharpness of your dancers' movements. I belong to the MTV generation that used to spend hours watching music videos and cartoons, and it all remains somewhere deep inside. There were pictures in my life that I will never forget. All of this comes together in my work, but what exactly inspires me is a good question. And yes, in a way, we really do silent movies, but sometimes I do want to talk. Language is important to me. Of course, I am very careful because you can ruin everything with words, so instead of words I use, for example, noises. When a dancer is making noises, this brings us back to an almost animal state. If we start quarrelling, with words we could go on forever without reaching a solution. Dance, too, can be misunderstood, but in dance you have no baseline to understand._____Referring to silent movies,

(pages 5, 8, 126–7, 130–1, 133, 260–1) Tué, 2014

I also meant the traits that have probably resulted from the technology available at the time, like the absence of smooth transitions between movements that renders each movement especially distinct. Similar traits are present in your choreography. Early in my career, I wanted to leave out everything I knew from other choreographers and just see what remained. I didn't want to use their ways of going from one step to another. I needed to get from A to B without anything I knew before, so it went from one frantic moment to the other in a very slapstick, absurd manner. Now it's becoming smoother, more generous. I allow myself a little bit of softness, but I still find it hard to do this in a 'dancy' way. I tie things up very strictly. I am very tough on myself by not letting other feelings, or other choreographers, enter my work._____In ballet, they say that legs are a structural part of the dance, and arms are its expressive part. You prefer to highlight the upper part of the body, while covering and often obscuring the legs. Are you trying to conceal the 'mechanics' of the process so that only the expression remains visible? I want to give dance more dignity. To me, naked legs is something too private to be exposed. I also relate to fashion. One of the most impressive fashion icons is the tuxedo suit that Yves Saint Laurent has designed for women, an enormously elegant and powerful piece. Somehow these tuxedos always appear in my work, because this is the kind of elegance I am looking for. Legs in dark pants connect to the floor and lengthen the body, as if it were the trunk of a beautiful tree, while the crown of this tree can be emotional, or wild, or silent. In fact, even with big ballerinas, what people look at when they step on stage is their upper body and their face. This is what we see first if we meet someone in real life. I find eyes, hands, and the back way more exciting than legs._____You treat darkness as a substance; a material from which you extract things by means of light. In your choreographic stories, light is a powerful motor. You must be working with it almost as much as you work with the movements. That is correct. I work with the lighting designer Udo Haberland, with whom we have done over forty pieces together. He comes to the studio by the time the piece is almost complete, in order to immerse it into his lighting and put everything together. The light is actually very simple, but there is a lot of work behind this simplicity, because on stage I usually only have people and empty space. Lighting is a big art. You have to go through a long-breath, passionate, frustrating technical process until you find the right dozes and transitions—and then, all of a sudden, it becomes meaningful and magical.

5

– conversion, metamorphosis, shift, changeover, renewal,

revolution, alteration, switch, transmutation, transfiguration

" How would you define ^the MATERIAL you work with ?

_____

Why have you chosen it ?

BILL VIOLA

BILL VIOLA

artist

How would you describe the materials you work with? Video for me was magical when I first encountered it. I was immediately fascinated by the cathode ray tube, a pale blue glow emitting from the monitor that produced miraculous images. I was also drawn to the 'live' aspect of video, an eye that is always open (surveillance cameras) that inspired many experimental works with 'open circuit' systems. For the first time also, I had a camera system that could record and play back instantly. Previously, this was only possible with Polaroid still photographs. Many tape delay pieces were created in this way, I had the ability to play with place and time. The video camera can often see more than the human eye, it becomes a surrogate eye for extended vision (telephoto), or close-up (macro), that provides me tools to make work that aligns with my interest in expressing our inner world._____Over the years the continuing development of media technology has enabled me to broaden my palette and to grow as an artist, expanding my resources that help me explore the themes that have been critical to my art. Video, or rather its digital child, can now replicate or 'invent' reality, it can seamlessly change speeds, it can go forward or backward, and it can also fit in your pocket._____However, video is simply a tool, the medium in which I work. My inspiration has come from

(pages 138–9) THE QUINTET OF THE ASTONISHED, 2000. Performers: John Malpede, Weba Garretson, Tom Fitzpatrick, John Fleck, Dan Gerrity :: (pages 142–3) EARTH MARTYR and FIRE MARTYR, 2014. Performers: Norman Scott (Earth Martyr), Darrow Igus (Fire Martyr)

I have come to realize that the most important place

where my work exists is not in the museum gallery,

or in the screening room, or on television, and not even

on the video screen itself, but _____*in the mind of the viewer*

who has seen it _____ ● In fact, **IT IS ONLY THERE THAT IT CAN EXIST** ●

Freeze a video in time and you are left with a single static

frame, isolated from context, an abandoned image, like

a butterfly under glass with a pin through it ● Yet, during

its normal presentation, viewers can only physically

experience video one frame at a time ● One can never

witness the whole all at once; by necessity it exists

only as a function of individual memory ● This paradox

gives video its living dynamic nature as part of the stream

of human consciousness ———

STATEMENT 1989

the words of the spiritual masters, through the many books I have collected and read over the years. It has also come from the many years spent in observation, in particular, of landscape, natural and urban; of human nature, the emotions; my family; and of perception and human consciousness._____You once said: "There has got to be a little space of emptiness in everything you do, and then it will live forever" . . . In the time that I spent in Japan observing master painters or highly skilled craftspeople at their work, I learned that if a piece comes close to perfection, then it needs to be subverted. A part of it will be altered so that it does not reach that ideal. There must always be a way to go forward, to continue developing an idea, or a creation. The Japanese have a word for the space in between—Ma—the space in between trees, for example, or buildings. My work needs to be open, to keep the mystery alive. The viewer is the missing part that completes the work, and his/her participation is as varied as there are viewers. Artists have followed the creative thread for thousands of years, each one inspiring the next. If there was perfection, there would be nothing to do for the new generation of artists. What kind of new capabilities do you believe people need to develop—or, rather, which limitations do we need to overcome—and how can art contribute to this evolution? Human beings evolve either via DNA, or through technology. Right now, technology is way ahead in this race. The fact that our ears can hear a telephone call from the other side of the world is not because we have developed super human hearing but we are using technology as an extension of ourselves. The trick is how to keep the technology from overtaking us. There has been for some time a lively and serious discussion about Artificial Intelligence and the danger of how it could cause the demise of the human race. A large part of the discussion is the question of what it means to be human. This is where art comes into the discourse. Artists are trying to define the human soul.

144

(facing) TRANSFIGURATION, 2007. Performer: Blake Viola

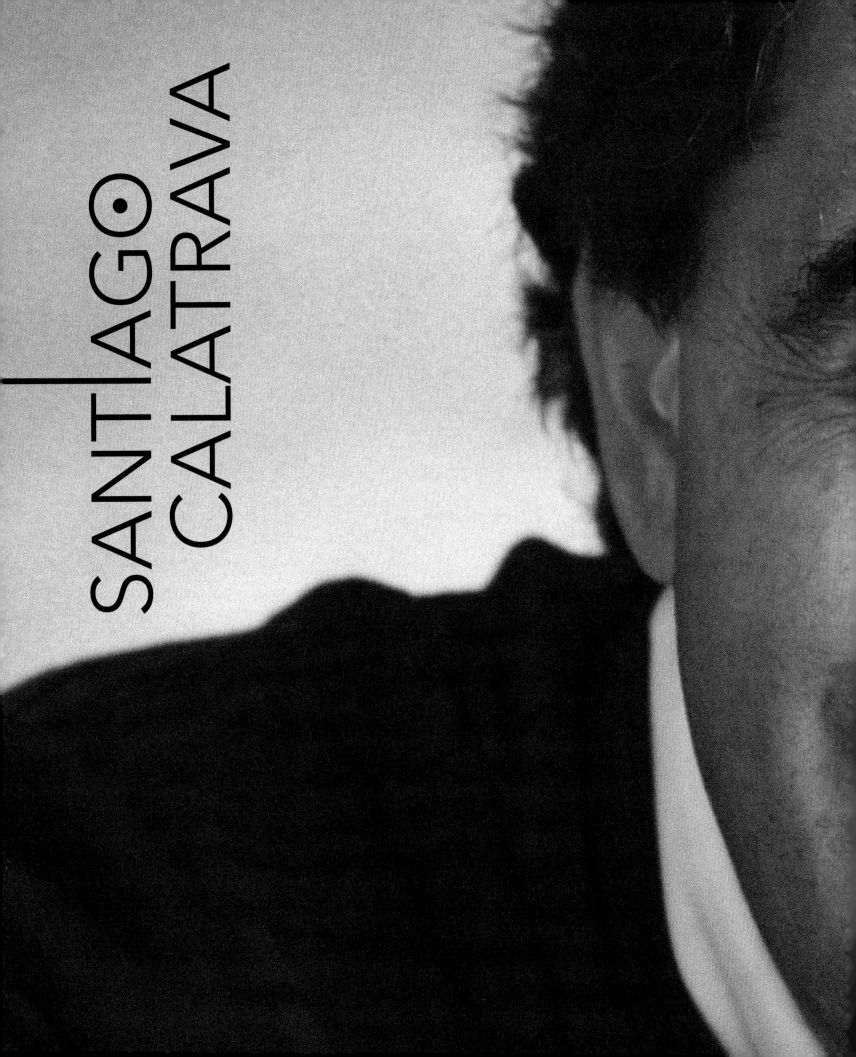

SANTIAGO CALATRAVA

SANTIAGO CALATRAVA

architect

You say that an architect can work with forces in the same way as a painter works with colours . . . We live in a universe in which light is reflected off every object to create the colours that we perceive, and in which gravity is the dominant force that governs us, the shape of trees, the waves of the sea and everything around us. The perception of these colours, translated by a painter's mind, leads to the Art of Painting. Similarly, gravitational forces are a subject matter for the architect to work with, which leads to the Art of Architecture._____**Apart from the forces, what other materials, in a wider sense, constitute your palette?** Architecture is not limited to a single material, and, in a way, it is almost intangible; it is the shape and the scheme that binds the materials. It is a kind of spiritual quality that you can give to the material in order to transform it into architecture through the force of the shadows, through the force of the chiaroscuro, all of which are derived through the force of Mother Nature._____**What about movement?** The idea of movement is implicit within the forces. It is also implicit within our lives, as our life occurs along a timeline. Without time, everything would stand still, and thus no movement would be possible. In this sense, movement and time are very closely related in our lives._____I mentioned before that forces are a subject matter for architecture. However, if we look at the forces purely from a static point of view, we are perhaps missing the fact that a force is physically the product of mass and acceleration, and in acceleration there is a cinematic value, in which time is implicit. This means that even in the 'force' the element of time is embedded._____If something does not move, it doesn't mean that it cannot move, as inherently there is a potential for movement trapped within it. This is where the idea of movement in architecture comes from; explicit movement or implicit movement, as much as the idea of movement in art, such as the expressive movement of the Greek sculptures, or the movement in dance. Those implicit movements are fundamental for the expression of the art and are a part of our existence, as of course architecture is a fundamental part of our existence, and likewise movement is a fundamental part of architecture._____You believe that new technologies allow

...in a way, *archi— tecture* is almost

intangible

(above and page 153) WORLD TRADE CENTER TRANSPORTATION HUB, New York City, 2016

architects to give a new dimension to buildings. What kind of dimension is it? 'Technology' is an ancient word that comes from the Greek vocabulary. 'Technique' derives from 'tekton', which means 'worker' and signifies a worker's skill to achieve something. Seeing it from this perspective is beautiful, because the Greeks related something as abstract as the technology to the man, who is the Tekton. In this way, the term becomes humanised. On the other hand, in the Ancient Greek language, 'tekton' has the same root as 'tekhné', which means 'art'. One might ponder then, what would be the inherent difference between 'technique' and 'art', if both words share the same origin? The difference is that one of them is able to move me. Hearing a beautiful piece of music can bring tears to my eyes; a beautiful building can generate within me an enormous emotional response. Through technology, we can also achieve and convey emotion. If this is truly achieved, then technique becomes art._____You compare architecture to a time capsule, calling it the most tangible sign of the civilisation. If we consider the bridges, the transportation hubs and other structures that you have designed as a message to the future, what would this message convey? Personally, I try to be inspired by the idea that architecture is a philanthropic exercise. You create these buildings in order to serve people by making their everyday lives easier. Beyond that, I would also like these people to experience a sense of beauty from architecture, because I deeply believe that beauty dignifies people's lives, and through a building's beauty you show people your respect, and share with them the idea that we are here to do better things than simply taking a train or sitting upon a chair. The uplifting aspect that architecture can bring into their lives is very important, particularly for those that are using a station everyday to go to work and perhaps are working in difficult conditions. Architecture can tell them: "This building is here for you with all of its services and all of its beauty." This is a very important part of the message I would like to convey.

MIGUEL CHEVALIER

(above) BELLA DONNA, FRACTAL FLOWERS series, 2009. Software: Cyrille Henry
(facing) SUR-NATURE, SEED n°1, 2004. Software: Music2eye

MIGUEL CHEVALIER

artist

Which scientific disciplines do you connect with in your work? I haven't studied science, but I find an extremely rich source of inspiration in the phenomena it describes. The installation *Liquid Pixels* [software: Cyrille Henry] was heavily inspired by the studies of turbulence and the mixing of fluids. *The Origin of the World* is a kind of psychedelic universe that draws upon the studies of the cellular automata. The colonies of cells that evolve, fuse or repel each other have provided ideas for this generative artwork, in which the processes never return to the original state. *Virtual Seeds* were born from my interest in agro engineering. Looking into the studies of plant growth, I decided to create imaginary plants that would emulate such processes. I'm also interested in the fractal theory. Thanks to Benoit Mandelbrot, the mathematician who has pointed out that the world is not as chaotic as it appears, we can now see some of its underlying structures. The *Fractal Flowers* are fictional plants based on growth simulation software, to which I have applied fractal algorithms. They have nothing to do with the botanical studies, but they allowed me to create an imaginary world that makes you reflect on what an artificial life form could be—not in the literal sense, of course, but as a form of procedural, self-generative life. The European Commission's Human Brain Project aims to simulate the brain and develop brain-inspired computers. I'm wondering if, in this extremely sophisticated neurobiological research, we will be able to identify some procedures that

Today is about the EVER— SELF—TRANS— FORMING works

that are never totally complete •

I could integrate in my artworks._____Self-generation is one of your recurring themes; what are the roots of this interest? Self-generating processes create extraordinary works that would have been impossible to realise otherwise. You just put the ingredients together, and it starts evolving on its own. Food for thought about the processes that give birth to new universes. Maybe that's what creation is: an encounter of multiple elements that are not significant on their own, whereas together they produce new, unthought-of ideas. Scientists use to have a rational, analytical approach, but sometimes they cross-breed seemingly incompatible things, and this leads to discovering new worlds._____In the times of hyper-specialisation, digital technologies allow us to build bridges between the domains that have drawn so wide apart since the age of the humanists, the geniuses like Leonardo da Vinci who were both scientists and artists. I came into technology because, as regards painting, my feeling was that the avant-gardists in the 20th century had explored all of the possible issues in graphic representation.

(above, top) THE ORIGIN OF THE WORLD at K11 Art Foundation, Shanghai 2014. Music: Jacopo Baboni Schilingi

(bottom) BINARY WAVE at La Fabrika Studio, Ivry-sur-Seine (France), 2011 :: Software for both projects: Cyrille Henry / Antoine Villeret

(above) CELESTIAL VAULTS at the Saint-Eustache church, Nuit Blanche, Paris 2016.
Software: Cyrille Henry / Antoine Villeret

I couldn't see where else a painter could find new original ideas. I was convinced that, in order to speak about the contemporary world, one had to use contemporary technologies and create poetic universes inspired by science. To me, being an artist today means being the explorer of hidden worlds, to highlight and animate them, and demonstrate how art can evolve on screen, but also at an architectural scale in a public space where it creates magic for people._____**Many of your works have a strong interactive and even immersive aspect . . .** What's more, viewers can influence an artwork's behaviour. This adds unprecedented qualities like engaging with potentiality, because, if you won't interact with the artwork either through body movements or through a tactile interface, you will only have a partial experience. Digital art is not at all in conflict with 19th- and 20th-century art. The Pointillist movement, which arose from Seurat's investigations and was inspired by Michel Eugène Chevreul's light diffraction theories, anticipated the cathode ray tube and the computer screen. Kinetic art's Victor Vasarely, Jesús Rafael Soto, François Morellet or Julio Le Parc, who researched optical phenomena and introduced the first forms of interactivity, were the precursors of the digital world. And, speaking of immersion, think of Monet's *Water Lilies*, in which he makes us 'enter' the painting that seems to transcend the bounds of its frame!_____**What is the relation between the 'finite' and the 'infinite' in your work?** Next to a process-based work, you can have 'finite' ones that are basically the screenshots of these processes. These 2D- and 3D-printed or digitally cut pieces materialise a frozen moment or a possible evolutionary step of an artwork. With the infinite, we focus on the evolution, while with the finite, a material presence is being created. Today, we are constantly experiencing this real-meets-virtual condition. We are having relationships with objects; we find ourselves simultaneously in the finite and in the infinite . . . One just has to have it both ways!

(facing) MAGIC CARPETS at Castel del Monte, Andria (Italy), 2014. Software: Cyrille Henry / Antoine Villeret

(above and facing) ALLEGORIA SACRA, the final part of the Liminal Space Trilogy, 2011–13

AES+F

artists + photographer :: page 165, left to right: Vladimir Fridkes (F),
Lev Evzovich (E), Tatiana Arzamasova (A), Evgeny Svyatsky (S)

Let's start with dissecting the art form you are working with. LEV EVZOVICH: Our visual language has always involved photographic image, portraits, multi-figure compositions, but one day we began playing with the scroll wheel, and suddenly a sequence of photos turned into funny motion pictures. Captivated by the bizarre effect, we decided to experiment with morphing the photos while slowing down the tempo. Partly due to limited source materials, our first attempt looked like poorly made animation, yet we came to appreciate those imperfections because they allowed us to further explore some of the subjects we've always been interested in, such as the deformation of faces and bodies, or the fine line between beauty and ugliness. We were particularly amused by the discrepancy of the audience reactions: the art world accepted it wholesale as a specific, intentionally developed language, while technology specialists accused us of sloppy work. As this new language evolved in subsequent projects, it grew simpler in some aspects and more sophisticated in the others, sometimes approaching cinematography, while at other times getting closer to subtly animated paintings. TATIANA ARZAMASOVA: Having opted for 'artificialised' movements, we maintained ties with painting in general and fresco in particular. Our works allow for a similarly prolonged perception; viewers can take time contemplating a certain emotion or movement. LE: These slow motion videos are based on creepy, limited, slightly unwholesome and thoroughly controlled movements

We seek to overcome SOCIAL, GENDER and all other kinds *of* **stereotypes**, *including* ridiculous cases *of* p litical c rrectness.

that are built from 10-second fragments. With morphing applied during post-production, you get characters that resemble robots rather than real people, which is exactly the effect we are aiming at. [TA:] Every large canvas captures a certain ritual. Each representation of Judith and Holofernes is a classical murder that we, the audience, scrutinise. Our work deals with social rituals, and yet it uses the same mythological allusions and iconic gestures, which, combined with slow, zombie-like movements, allow the viewer to recognise and absorb what is going on._____You say that your method was born from an accident, but it is surely one of those accidents that trigger the things which have been laying dormant. [LE:] The idea of adding movement was completely natural to our evolution within the framework of photography. Both intuitively and consciously, we sought to enhance our language. From digital collage that blurred the distinctions between the real and the virtual, our next step was to add the dimension of time. Documentary video, filmed performance didn't work for us; even filming in a studio failed to respond to our aesthetics of extreme artificiality. We had multiple reasons to prefer photography to filming. In terms of resolution, the capacity of a photo camera is still unbeatable. In addition to combining different images—something that the film industry, too, is perfectly capable of doing—it offers the unique possibility to shoot a full figure, then zoom its face and use it as a portrait in the final cut. Unlike in film or

(above) LAST RIOT, the first part of the *Liminal Space Trilogy*, a video installation and a series of stills, drawings and sculptures, 2005–07
(facing) INVERSO MUNDUS, a multi-channel video installation and a series of stills and digital collages, 2015

in traditional video, at the shooting stage we only produce 'constructs', while everything else, even certain storylines, is created during the montage. Besides, high resolution photography enables a specific ambience that looks as if all air had been pumped out. As a result, the foreground and the background are perceived with equal sharpness in that artificial world that seems to be made of plastic . . . Something that we like a lot. Why? LE: Because we love working with cliches and stereotypes. We are obsessed with flawless surfaces. We want the spectator to feel like piercing this glossy surface to see what it hides. Our work has to annoy. TA: In the constructed reality of our videos, we achieve the unrealistic degree of sharpness that feels almost painful. It is not even beautiful; it's sickeningly crisp, which makes you see things differently. LE: Working with the notion of beauty is something rare in contemporary art where beauty is regarded as an ambiguous territory. Where is that fine line? How do we appropriate the commercial image? What is really beautiful? And what does 'really beautiful' even mean? Those are the questions we like to ask._____Your work focuses on threshold spaces and states . . . LE: In fact, *Liminal Space* is the name of the trilogy. In *Allegoria Sacra*, an allusion to Bellini's painting, the airport serves as Purgatory. *Last Riot* depicts a massacre in which not a single drop of blood is being shed. In *Trimalchio*, pleasure morphs into depression. TA: The outcome is never shown. Our Judith just brings her sword to Holoferne's throat—and, since every gesture already belongs to the realm of mythology, the viewer's mind completes the movement. LE: *Inverso Mundus*, the project that followed the *Liminal Space Trilogy*, equally deals with the transitional state in which all and everything find themselves today. The romantic futurism has ceased to be. There is no sense of linear progress, only incessant fluctuation between different values. An ongoing in-between state. TA: The end of a myth as the beginning of another one.

172

(facing) THE FEAST OF TRIMALCHIO, the second part of the *Liminal Space Trilogy*, 2009–10

6

TRANSCENDENCE

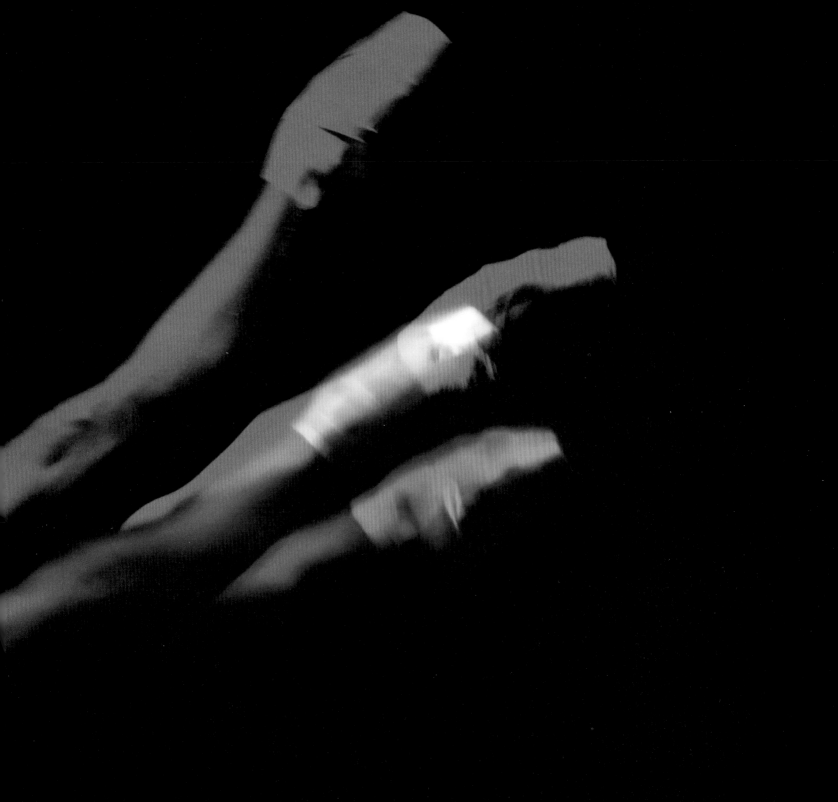

BEYOND YOUR OWN CREATIVE DOMAIN,
WHICH OTHERS ARE YOU LOOKING INTO ?

EDOUARD
LOCK

EDOUARD LOCK

contemporary dance choreographer

Information processed when observing someone move is too great to offer more than a partial understanding of the detail involved. Data necessary to define proportion, shape, gender and other specifics is more easily obtained when the body is static, and becomes exponentially more difficult when movement is introduced. Which makes of the moving body an abstract. This abstract is, in my opinion, well suited to reveal more of our nature than the body seen as a social, gender or other symbol._____**You considered being a writer, but finally opted for choreography . . .** It seems to me that a connection exists between language and movement. Language isn't just a tool used to facilitate precise communication. It's also an aesthetic construct where cadence, rhythm and structures that govern the way words are brought together, pronounced and sound all form important elements that define a language. These structural elements have less to do with meaning and more to do with a set of aesthetic preferences that have coalesced over time, habit and history. Similarly, choreography is not at its best as the bearer of a precise narrative, but also defines itself through choices involving cadence, body shape, movement detail and myriad other elements that are not only narrative specific._____Words are used to define and order the world, and seem interchangeable with the things that they represent. Yet words do not contain complete information about what they refer to. As an example, the word 'red' does not contain any relevant information as to the nature or characteristics of that colour that would help someone who has never

(pages 61, 174–5, 180–1, 183) <u>*New Work*</u> *(2010)*

seen it understand. The word 'body' contains as little information about its subject as the word 'red'. Once the link between a word and what it represents is established, however, they seem to be able to alter and influence each other by reordering the information they refer to in new ways. Much as the body and the movement it hosts do._____Choreography reaches beyond the pure functionality of movement, but I'd say that you also try to go beyond its aesthetic component. What is your destination then? Aesthetics in some ways implies one specific view or perception of the body over another. Might it then not be more interesting and accurate for choreography to present the body as a sum of details too great to understand? To use choreography to veil rather than reveal and in so doing infer that an absolute understanding of the body is impossible. To point out that if the body is too complex to be understood, then it is also too complex to carry only one narrative or iden-tity._____Nature has a selfish level of detail that does not adapt its complexity to the onlooker and as a result has a greater scope of possibilities than what the observer expects, or can use._____Memories of ourselves accumulated at different points in our lives and for different reasons interact with each other to create a composite self image. A set of virtual bod-ies that we use, interact with and exchange to suit our needs. These virtual bodies modifying and replacing each other influence how we perceive ourselves. One set of physical definitions replaces the other in sometimes fluid, sometimes fragmented ways. This could be of interest to choreographers because if the above is right, the body as an object in flux and at rest has

179

WE PERCEIVE THE WORLD

symbolically

,

■

MEANING THAT SOMETIMES

WE DON'T see THE WORLD

an undefined set of characteristics that make it both a symbol, a memory and a complex structure. *In your filmed works, such as Velasquez or Amelia, you change perspectives and radically shift the coordinate system, making us realise that we have had a totally wrong idea of the space we were looking at. Why and how is the space important to you?* Normally, the space defines the activity, but on stage it's the dancer that defines the space, which reacts to the dancer's activity and becomes fluid. Space on stage is an allegory for the world. A sort of reactive architecture. An enclosure where we extend our subjective reality into the world as much as the world intrudes into us. As such, space is charged with intent and becomes a receptacle for the audience's projection. It is a host in which choreography can 'live'._____*How do you create the connection between the dancers and the audience?* There are two types of approaches. With a charismatic approach, a performer steps on stage and says, "I look good; I dance well; I am certainly able to do that thing better than you are. So sit down, look at me, get pleasure from this, and then leave." With the empathetic theatre, performers go on the edge of their control; they are inviting failure on stage. And when they do that, they connect to the audience in a strong way, because audiences have no exit doors, no wings. So when they see an artist saying, "I have to solve a problem, and I am not sure I can," this initiates hope, because it's the same dynamics as found in real life. It's a more fragile way of doing it, but the links between the dancer and the audience are also more real stated that way than in a charismatic performance where the audience passively looks on._____*You argue that creation is a listening process. Yet, at a certain point, you need to share what you have heard with others. How does this transition happen?* When you first get an idea, it's abstract, vague, undefined even to oneself. You can sense its pulse, its nascent shape, but it remains hidden and too complex to fully frame or communicate. In order to understand it, this 'proto-idea' needs to be simplified even to oneself. As it's communicated to others, the simplification continues, so that if the aim is to have everyone understand the same thing from that first thought, then there is the risk that the original idea will be denatured and simplified. I would suggest that sharing is most effective when it leaves some doubt as to the nature and intent of the thought being communicated.

MOSES
PENDLETON

MOSES PENDLETON

contemporary dance choreographer, artistic director, photographer

188 The Earth is trying to keep us from flying out; gravity is like a seatbelt. Ballet is based on changing the sense of gravity. It recreates the structure of the body to be a bird, responding to the basic urge to escape the heaviness of our world. We offer MOMIX as a kind of escape, a fantasy that is an integral part of our reality._____**Your pieces are not human-centred, or rather not person-centred. I'd say that you feel totally unrestricted about the different creatures, objects or even ideas a dancer can be turned into.** Through the body and the brain we are connected to the things beyond the human. Humans are great imitators and in their genetic codes they have swans, turtles, snails, monsters and angels. It may feel threatening to some, but it's all in us. I see this and try to animate everything that surrounds us on Earth, of which humans are just a part._____Making a contact with the natural world is the primary point. On a day like this *[a frosty February day in a snow-covered forest in Washington, Connecticut]*, I'd walk three or four hours. Long walks in a frozen landscape will affect my thinking. You are getting energised like a solar battery, because the sun is never more radiant than on a snow day when its glare is amplified by the white snow._____Living in the country, you can be alone, but you are not lonely at all. I socialise with my own imagination and with the things that are not human. I can fall in love with an oak tree; it's a big experience that is not so different from falling in love with a pretty girl in high school. I'm looking for infatuations with the surprising armature of an old ash tree; I'm looking for the body of an oak tree—the back, the arm,

(pages 187, 191, 193) <u>*F.L.O.W.*</u> *(2010) :: (pages 186, 190) photographs by Moses Pendleton*

making the new **boxes** to think *outside of*

the leg, the dance. In what I have photographed, you don't see a flower, but the dancer in the flower, and maybe you will see the flower in the dancer, so it's crossing over from the human to the non-human._____I'm very involved with taking pictures. I do micro-photography of ice and snow, and I'd like to give crows credit for some of my best photographs. One of my favourites is a picture of a crow's droppings in a puddle, frozen into an elegant, Loïe Fuller-like dance. Could be the poster for a ballet._____**How do you translate an image into a physical act, a dance?** Physical acts come first. For example, when we created Diana's piece on a mirror, we played around with reflection not yet knowing what it was. Suddenly you start seeing a nude doubled in the mirror, as an echo of Narcissus. Lisa Gerrard's music, her spiritual sensuality was an important player in the overall effect of this solo on the glass. I took a lot from the song where she sings about a longing for her sensual self and yet feeling that love from above is pulling her up. In the end, [Diana's character] becomes a hermaphrodite, a strange alien creature that goes down into the lake. We improvise with shapes and movements; we sketch, and every sketching session is videotaped. After you have played, you can become analytical, and maybe out of those five minutes you will get 30 seconds of good material, and find a logical move to the next thing in that picture. We construct it like a sculpture or a painting. A path originates from not knowing where to go, but once you have this path, the dancers can be their own artists; they can interpret the breath of Lisa Gerrard with an elbow, so that in the end you don't even want to see a woman in the mirror, you just want to sense this mystical song. That would be ideal. As Balanchine would say, "this dance made me see the music for

the first time."_____I'm not seeing images; I'm looking for them. I'm an image-maker. What is an image, a prop, a costume? What are we trying to make that will fulfil a painterly, a sculptural satisfaction, and then move it through time and space, and turn it into a dance? A lot of choreographers work on dance steps, but steps are the last thing in my case; it's the image first. If I'm doing something about the garden and want to turn a woman into a flower, we get a petticoat, multiply it by four to create a big puffball, dye it orange, and when the lights come up, you are looking at marigolds! What we spend time on is developing costumes that will make five female MOMIX dancers look like marigolds. It's a beautiful device of changing: as you slowly move your costume from your head down your body, it changes the look of the dance. At a certain height, it is a samba skirt, and when this little puffball is finally at the bottom, it turns into a magic carpet and makes a perfect way for the dancer to turn into a 'marigold fairy', an elemental, and disappear._____The artistic sensibility is in the curiosity and fascination of looking at something and seeing more than just that. Picasso would look at the junk that people had thrown away and see that if he took a broken bicycle seat and handlebars and put them together on the wall, it would be the Minotaur. He didn't do a lot of work on it, but what his mind saw [is essential here]. You have to know that it is a bicycle seat and still see the Minotaur at the same time. When you put it up on the wall, you are giving it to the world, and then people can make it different by their perception. It will keep changing with other people's attention and other interpretations._____**An artist can also directly experiment with the viewer's perception. There are pieces that use sound or light to radically alter our experience of a space or an object's shape and therefore add a few extra dimensions to our concept of the world that surrounds us.** Musician Brian Eno says that the new theatre for him will be just creating glass structures that can play with light and playing the music in a surround sound system. The audience will drift and daydream, and that will be the show. That's my job; I try to walk through the day as if in a trance, but not totally so—in this way, you can remember it later. I still have the obligation to try to bring back the research and share it with the general human public.

7

en
S O U L
ment

—the moment in which a being gains a soul.

"What is it that makes a being alive?

AITOR THROUP

(above) Throup's garments, accessories and art direction in a shoot for *Vogue Hommes* Japan, 2012
(facing) a digital portrait of Damon Albarn for his first single EVERYDAY ROBOTS, 2014

AITOR THROUP

artist, designer and creative director

. . .I strongly believe that 'what is art?' is an unanswerable question. Art is a way of communicating through infinite non-pre-established systems, while language is an established and extremely limited system of communication. As we evolve, more and more often we will communicate without language—through art, dance, music. I am trying to develop my own systems of communicating certain ideas that have moral, philosophical, practical and definitely personal reasons to exist. For me, 'reason' is the most important word. My goal is to only create things that exist for a reason. Sometimes they are arguably not better in the traditional sense, but they unlock new opportunities. **You say that you want the garments to move with the wearer, rather than the wearer moving inside of them. This brings us very close to a garment merging with the body, or acting as a body extension.** I have been interested in anatomy since I was very young. My mother was trained to be a doctor, and I was a witness to medical imagery from an early age. Besides, for a child of my age, I could make technically advanced drawings. These two factors evolved into me being able to draw a human body, particularly in motion, which led to an interest in connecting it to clothing as an extension of the body. My earliest clothing-related memory is a recurring dream I have had since the age of nine. I was at sea, and a box was floating away from me. More than anything else, I wanted to get closer and understand the thing that was in the box, but it just floated

as a DESIGNER, I answer the *questions* posed by *myself* as an ARTIST

away. I knew what was in there: Batman's mask from Tim Burton's 1989 film. That was the impact of the first time I watched the film; the moment that Michael Keaton's character sees the mask looking at him. This hollow object has sculpted his face and exaggerated his features. Later I realised that it was product design used to create a piece of art, because that's what art is—communicating an entire story in one product, be it a painting, a musical piece, or a film. The whole story was there, capturing the character's childhood fears and all. He didn't even need to be inside for the mask to communicate his personality. I became obsessed with the idea of capturing someone's soul in a product; in giving a product a soul without needing a person inside it._____The England football kit, designed for Umbro for the World Cup 2010, articulated and mimicked the way the body works as if it were a second skin. In my more extreme jackets from *New Object Research,* layered

(facing) stills from LEGS, a film by Aitor Throup and Ken-Tonio Yamamoto, 2010
(above, top) the DEATH VEIL MASK for the musician Flying Lotus, 2014 :: (bottom) a portrait of the Swedish actor Noomi Rapace, 2014

skins capture the human body. This helps to create a deep connection with the viewer. As we know, the most powerful way to trigger our reaction is to use a human figure, because we recognise ourselves in it as in a mirror. I am interested in masks, gloves and articulations as the anatomical functions depicted in products and objects. However, there is also a spiritual side to the anatomy; this is why we respond at a deeper level to an 'anatomical' work, and not necessarily a figurative one. It can even be a product design with exposed anatomy, like Dyson's revolutionary transparent vacuum cleaner. We connect with such objects because they—just like us—depend on many systems that work together towards just existing. I think of the pieces like Marc Quinn's *Self*, the artist's head cast from his own frozen blood. It is suspended in time yet fully dependent on the refrigeration system and the protective glass case. These anatomical pieces are complex systems that are, in fact, quite fragile and therefore remind us of ourselves. And I believe that my ultimate aim is to create pieces that truly have an anatomy._____Have you ever considered zooming even further into the garment's structure? That is, designing materials with specific qualities? Some of the first pieces in *New Object Research* have been created with hybrid materials developed in our studio for the pure purpose of giving the material itself an anatomy. When we use standardised solutions, our brain stops questioning and just accepts what we see. The purpose of newness is to stop us in our tracks and make us think. When I was a student, the way I stitched every piece had to follow my own methodology of stitching; I wanted to develop my own buttonholes, my own fastenings and cord locks . . . The ultimate goal for my pieces is to have a deep sense of new in their every aspect. Then there is no way that your mind gets lazy.

204

OLAFUR
ELIASSON

(above) RIVERBED, Louisiana Museum of Modern Art, Humlebæk (Denmark), 2014
(facing, top) CONTACT, Fondation Louis Vuitton, Paris, 2015 :: (facing, bottom) YOU SEE ME, installation view at Studio Olafur Eliasson, 2006

OLAFUR ELIASSON
artist

You call art 'a reality machine', referring to the potential it has for 'producing reality'. We share the responsibility for co-producing reality—as viewers, as artists, as citizens, as humans. There is an inherently cooperative element to this; you can't have reality without another person or a wider environment. When I make a work of art, I think of that artwork as having the potential to produce reality. But the artwork alone is not enough. It is only through the coming together of artwork and viewers in a certain situation that art co-produces reality._____**What kinds of materials do you work with?** The material I use most is actually *de*-material. I try to create situations where the work disappears as a stable thing in itself, where it is more about the fragile contract between the work as experience and the person who is experiencing it. In this sense, a work can simply be a feeling. Take my Little Sun lamp: on the one hand, it is a small solar-powered lamp in the shape of a sun; on the other hand, it is a social business engaged in spreading light and prosperity to some of the 1.2 billion people worldwide who don't have access to electricity. Ultimately, for me though, it is a feeling. When I was developing Little Sun together with the engineer Frederik Ottesen, we asked ourselves how it feels to have power. Little Sun is more about the feeling of holding energy in your hands than it is about a material thing that conveys this feeling. **Many of your works can only be experienced in motion; you even use the tagline 'you**

being *alive* means having DIRECT CON— SEQUENCES for our *surroundings*

only see things when you move'. Why is movement so important to you? We are all constantly in motion, and even when we stand still, everything else is moving. The world we live in is not composed of static, monolithic images, but of things that are changing, shifting, flowing. Since movement unfolds temporally, it brings together space and time. According to Henri Bergson, 'movement is reality itself'. In the case of art, movement introduces individual, subjective perspectives. As I move around a work of art, it changes. I co-produce the aesthetic experience that is art. Your works create a kind of suspension by altering our habitual patterns of perception. What kind of awareness do you want this experience to bring out? My hope is to help people become actively aware that the world is made up of an agglomeration of causal

(facing) YOUR ATMOSPHERIC COLOUR ATLAS, 21st Century Museum of Contemporary Art, Kanazawa, 2009
(above) BEAUTY, Moderna Museet, Stockholm, 1993

relationships, that things are never simple or stable, and that this complexity and instability depends on our presence and our subjectivity. Things reverberate with different meanings from one discourse, one set of thoughts or visions, to the next. My work brings to the surface the ways this knowledge is embodied, already present within us, and only needs to be uncovered and examined. It's an awareness of the awareness we already have. **Which scientific disciplines do you involve in developing your projects?** I find great inspiration in science, but, generally, I look at science from a non-specialist point of view. I do not translate scientific ideas or theories into artworks, but rather begin from a feeling or intuition and develop the work pragmatically through doing. In my studio in Berlin, I work with a diverse group of architects, engineers, art historians, cooks, designers, videographers, educators, computer programmers and skilled craftsmen. For many years, I collaborated closely with the architect and mathematician Einar Thorsteinn. I worked with the geologist Minik Rosing to create *Ice Watch* in City Hall Square in Copenhagen, to raise awareness about the urgent need for action on climate change. I am also deeply inspired by the work of the neuroscientist Tania Singer, who is researching compassion and mindfulness; what I have learned from her research has influenced my recent thinking and projects, works like the app *Your exhibition guide* (2014), and the web-based work *Moon* (2013), made in collaboration with Ai Weiwei._____**What makes a being, an artwork alive?** Artworks, like people, are alive when they are in contact with the world. Being alive means having direct consequences for our surroundings. The challenge is to be aware of what these consequences are. This is why artworks insist on our engagement, and why, layered in a complex mesh of relations with other things, people and environments, they can change the world.

214

RAFFAELLO
d'ANDREA

(above) The ROBOTIC CHAIR, made in collaboration with Max Dean and Matt Donovan, looks like an ordinary chair but can pull itself back together after falling apart, 2006
(facing) CUBLI, a collaboration with ETH Zurich, is a cube with a side length of 15 cm (5.9 in) that can jump up and balance on its corner, 2013

RAFFAELLO D'ANDREA

engineer, artist, entrepreneur

220   In the process of creating robots and even entire systems whose members cooperate, learn and adapt, you are probably getting closer to the (elusive) definition of consciousness. One may say that you are exploring alternative life forms and, in doing so, may have arrived at a new, updated concept of what it means to be alive. In many ways, these creations do appear to be alive. They are autonomous, they interact with their environment, they possess agency. The recent work by neuroscientists Tononi and Koch would, in fact, attribute some form of consciousness to these creations via what is known as Integrated Information Theory, which is very much related to the philosophy of panpsychism, or the view that there is a spectrum of consciousness. This intuitively makes sense by considering the alternative: for example, if we are conscious, and the two cells that we all started from are not, when exactly did we reach consciousness? Clearly there is a spectrum of consciousness, and if this applies to biological life, why not everything else?_____You have once said that you and your team 'only build things that do not exist,' and that you don't think about applications but rather about pushing boundaries. How do you decide what you want to create?

I want to__CREATE things__*that are* IMPOSSIBLE

‾

What I really want to create are things that are impossible, which in itself is a contradiction. I want to create magic. Everything is my inspiration, and my medium is motion._____You say that you make no distinctions between 'artistic' and 'applied' projects, because all of them are equally about creating new things. The word 'art' is loaded, and its meaning is constantly changing, so it is difficult to say what is art and what is not. More importantly, why bother trying? Ultimately, what matters is that the things we create have value, and by this I don't mean in a purely economic sense, but rather in a societal sense (which encompasses economic utility)._____Adaptive robots that learn from making mistakes—just like humans and animals—are known to be much less expensive than those whose functioning is based on extreme precision. This is another proof that

(top) The SWINGING BLIND JUGGLER, a collaboration with ETH Zurich, can juggle balls without seeing them, and without catching them—that is, with zero sensory feedback, 2011 :: (bottom) A Quadrocopter juggling a ball in the FLYING MACHINE ARENA, a testing ground for mobile robots at ETH Zurich, 2011

FLIGHT ASSEMBLED ARCHITECTURE, measuring 6 m in height and composed of 1500 polystyerne bricks, is the first installation built by flying machines and developed in collaboration with Gramazio & Kohler architects as a model of their conceptual 'vertical village', a mega-structure that comprises an entire town, 2011

nature provides us with some of the most practical and pragmatic solutions. How often do you find direct inspirations in nature? Nature inspires me, but never directly. In particular, I don't try to directly duplicate strategies found in nature, it would be too restrictive. Having said that, we are creatures of nature, and it is clear that the way we think, the way we reason, is heavily influenced by it and our everyday experiences. Neuroscientists argue that, even if Artificial Intelligence beats human brain in terms of performance, the biggest (and apparently, unbridgeable) difference between them is that Artificial Intelligence can't be creative. This may mean that creativity would be 'the last recourse' in the humans' competition with Artificial Intelligence. I would tend to agree, but I would be careful with the word 'unbridgeable'. Never say never! What is clear is that we are extremely far away from creating a machine that displays creativity. But even if we did (or when we do), that would not be a bad thing for human beings, because it would push us to be creative at a higher level. I see machine creativity as a tool, rather than a threat.

(facing) SPARKED, a short film made in collaboration with Verity Studios, Cirque du Soleil and ETH Zurich, features a human actor interacting with a group of flying machines. The film uses no computer-generated imagery, wires, slow-motion or fast-forwards, 2014

_*Humans* will NEVER (!) become OBSOLETE

KNIGHT
CK

(above) ALEXANDER McQUEEN, 1997 :: (facing) DOLLS, SHOWstudio, 2000

(page 232) SEVEN DEADLY SINS, Mariacarla Boscono, 2016 :: (page 233) TRANSHUMAN AFTER ALL, VMAN, 2013

NICK KNIGHT

imagemaker

If you are standing in front of a shut door and know there is something exciting on the other side, why not open it? I see my work as opening doors._____I have always considered all art communication, and communication can be expressed in any form. With technologies allowing an easier access to media, the idea of cross-boundary work is very current today. You no longer have to do things the way you were always told they should be done, because now there are different ways of doing it. There are new tools for making art and new ways of interacting with people. The Internet, which is still in its infancy, is the single biggest communication adventure the world has ever seen. It changes fundamentally the relationship between the art and the artist; the artist and the audience. You can write a book and put it online. I can put a picture up in a matter of seconds, and people will see it. I rest open-eyed in front of the huge range of possibilities that are now out there. We can don a pair of glasses and find ourselves in somebody else's environment, which is interactive. People are living in a different dimension. The customisations they are starting to do of their lives and of themselves are fascinating. It starts feeling natural so quickly that you don't even realise that things have radically changed. It's like trying to make sense of an explosion that you can't see; you just feel the shock waves. It is easier to express than to analyse. We are in the middle of a change that shapes our society more than anything ever has in the past. Of course, it will bring forward new forms of art, new purposes for creating it, and new destinations. The much expected Internet of Things—basically, a kind of language that will allow everything to understand everything else—promises a different level of interaction and interconnection between humans and things. I can't think of a better time for working. People who previously wouldn't have been able to do it are now allowed into creating art. You no longer classify yourself, but just follow what you feel naturally drawn to. There is a growing realisation that lots more is possible. Imagine artificial intelligence involved in the creation of new forms, new art, new sounds. A lot of the traffic on the

WE ARE ENTERING a new phase in our development *as a species*

internet is for robots, so maybe we would also be thinking about the robotic audience? There is an absolutely new door ahead of us._____For you, the era of photography ended in the 1990s. Your Internet-based SHOWstudio was founded in 2000 with the goal of participating in the new era of what you call imagemaking. For the over 150 years that photography existed, it was a clearly defined medium. By the middle of the '90s, we got digital imaging; you could treat images as if they were paint. That was outside the parameters of photography. Then, in the late '90s, came the Internet that was the right platform to this new medium. SHOWstudio was intended as a place to do work unconfined by old structures; the platform for a new age. Internet allowed me to have a relationship with the audience, a two-way discourse that was much closer to the way we think. Our thought patterns are not revelations delivered from a pedestal. I didn't want art to be so expensive and rarefied; it had to feel alive. I found that people

in fashion—Alexander McQueen, Yohji Yamamoto, John Galliano and the generation that followed—were more artistic than anywhere else. What they were doing was not about outfits, but about some sort of burning passion that I didn't see in the art world where big galleries looked like banks. I grew up in the '70s, when punk happened, and you'd literally write across your chest what you thought. You became your own living piece of art. That's what fashion is: one of the most accessible, profound, pure forms of self-expression. One of the first things you do to remove people's personalities is to put them all in the same clothes. Most people see fashion as a commercial domain, but it's not how I treat it, and I wanted SHOWstudio to reflect that._____**You once spoke about that moment in a photo shoot when, after meticulous preparation, you finally press the button. This is the only moment you do not see. In other words, the whole process culminates in letting go of control?** It is only by losing control that you can have the freedom to see new possibilities. Imagemaking cannot be rehearsed. It is spontaneous and intuitive; it relies not on what you see, but on what you feel. As you press the button without knowing what there is, you work in a predictive state. It is also a very addictive state, in which you feel powerful; problems go away; you lose the recognition of your physicality. You see and feel things with faculty and intelligent reflection. It's a metaphysical state that may last a few seconds, or minutes. It can't be switched on; you can only do it through failure and chaos. It's hard to work in that cha-otic, accidental space, but that's where we should be. The surrealists used to paint their dreams; they believed that they were working with the unconscious mind. I believe in the conscious mind, but it has to be unaffected and unstructured._____**What makes a work alive?** What makes it alive is when it's based on something you couldn't previously understand and shows the things you haven't seen before.

(facing) DEVON, ALEXANDER McQUEEN, 1997

234

8

LIBERATION

IN YOUR ART, WHAT IS FREEDOM ?

(above) <u>*In the Middle, Somewhat Elevated*</u>
(facing) <u>*Black Flags*</u> *installation features two industrial robots whose movements are controlled by a digital algorithm and appear "unpredictable, weightless and measured at one and the same time", 2014*

WILLIAM FORSYTHE

contemporary dance choreographer, artist

What does 'thinking choreographically' mean? You could even say, behaving choreographically, or making choreographically. I work with visual arts a lot; you can see me as a visual artist that works in the medium of choreography, while my friend Antony Gormley is a choreographer that works in the medium of visual arts. His entire oeuvre is a very long, sustained choreography, which he goes through, frame by frame._____Dancing is a form of making, while choreography is suggesting. I can only make a suggestion for a possible outcome; it's like a mathematical proposition. Then the dancer suggests a realisation. Traditionally, we call it an interpretation, but in my case I work with problem-solving. I give dancers problems, and they have to invent solutions in real time._____**You emphasise that choreography and dance are two distinct practices.** They are two different things, but there is a condition where they can overlap. I don't know if dance is always choreographic, but choreography is not always dance-related. I don't know what causes us to identify a movement as dance; every culture has different criteria about what is considered dance. In certain cultures, there is dance, but no concept of choreography._____**What do you think of the definition of choreography as 'the art of designing sequences of movements'?** That would be one facet. Choreography is, in a sense, designing the probability of an outcome within an action, but there is no guarantee, because not everyone in the room comes from identical cultural backgrounds, and all expectations are not equal. The only thing I can know about is what I do myself. It might be something people don't care about, but it could be also, "oh, I didn't know you could do this with ballet!"_____I was once having a very difficult public discussion after a piece. There was an argument, and one dramatist said: "Art is . . ." And I said: "Stop, stop, stop! If you tell us what it is, the whole thing is over!" Imagine a dictionary, in which the definitions continuously evolve. The whole purpose of a practice is to invalidate the previous definitions as the only possible ones. This applies to visual arts, too. When Marcel Duchamp put his urinal out there, the reaction was, "It's not art", and he said: "Yes, it is". He questioned the notion of standard definitions. In his famous work called *Three Standard Stoppages*, he took a metre of string, held it a metre above the floor, then dropped it—and considered the form and the length of the string to be the new metre. In a sense, he was imitating the evolution of ideas, because the metre had no standard definition. It's an invention, as are all our ideas about aesthetics; they are inventions that rest on the shoulders of previous inventions. Something like the metre has entered into the domain of precision that transpires the anatomic level; it's at the level of physics *[today, the metre is defined as the distance travelled by light in vacuum during a time interval of one 299,792,458th of a second]*, while beforehand it used to be one ten-millionth of the distance from the Equator to the North Pole. An arabesque now and 100 years ago are two very different things. Things do change, and part of it is due to artists like Sylvie Guillem, or Diana who change the idea of how these could be done. Rene Magritte, the painter, said that "an object is not so possessed by its own name that one could not find another or better there-fore". A practice is not so possessed by its historical precedence that one could not find other or different ways to practice, just because it was done in a certain way until a certain point.

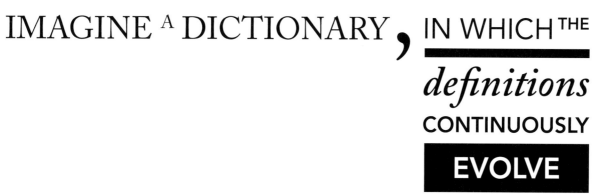

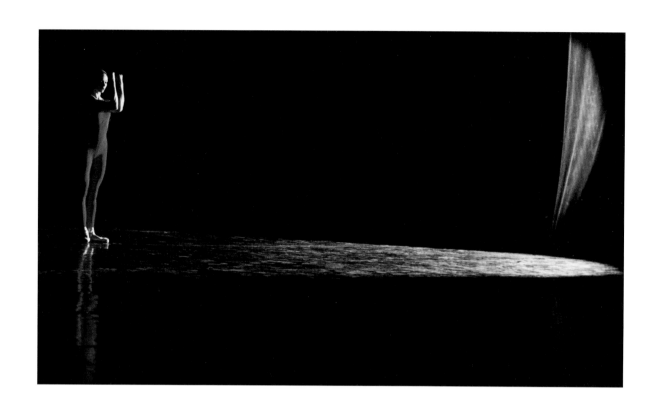

(above) <u>*In the Middle, Somewhat Elevated*</u>
(facing) <u>*Nowhere and Everywhere at the Same Time*</u>

How would you define the materials you work with? Time and sensation. There was a commentary about choreography not being an art form, but part of entertainment and dance. It can also be entertainment and dance, but does it have to be excluded because of the certain ways it has been practiced up till now, or could it be otherwise conceived? I do believe it is now being otherwise conceived. Many visual artists are now working in something close to choreography, if not choreography itself._____**Why have you gotten involved with plastic arts?** Because I didn't know you couldn't. I had a wonderful mentor who only said one sentence to me. After I did my first piece in high school, he took me to the side and said in a quiet whisper: "There are no rules." I didn't know any rules, I just did what I thought was right. When I created my first concert dance piece in the university, my teacher told me that I was not going to be a dancer, but a choreographer. I was confused and a little bit wary; I didn't think of myself as a choreographer, even though I had been choreographing since I was fourteen. **Designing sequences?** Improvising sequences. I usually organised improvisations within a framework. That's how I could think; that was the best use of my mind._____**When you ask a question, the answer comes in the form of movement?** By moving one can inform oneself about other fields of discourse. The actual experience and the metaphoric strength of certain contexts that one encounters through the body are a way of knowing certain things. It's valuable. I can't tell you why, but it seems to unlock certain conceptual domains._____**Probably, this is the reason why you are trying to identify the underlying principles in choreography that would apply to other domains.** I would like to assume that all organisations have affinities. It's interesting for me to see if I could find the linguistic properties of those affinities and see what language is shared. I looked at the counterpoint, for example, as one of the things that is most frequently shared in practices. It is used in hip hop, in ballet, in numerous dance organisations. Maybe I could make other kinds of organisations come into a different focus if they are represented with an analysis of our fundamentals—for example, of the counterpointed organisations in dance. So maybe we will illuminate other practices.

(facing) _The Defenders, Part 1_

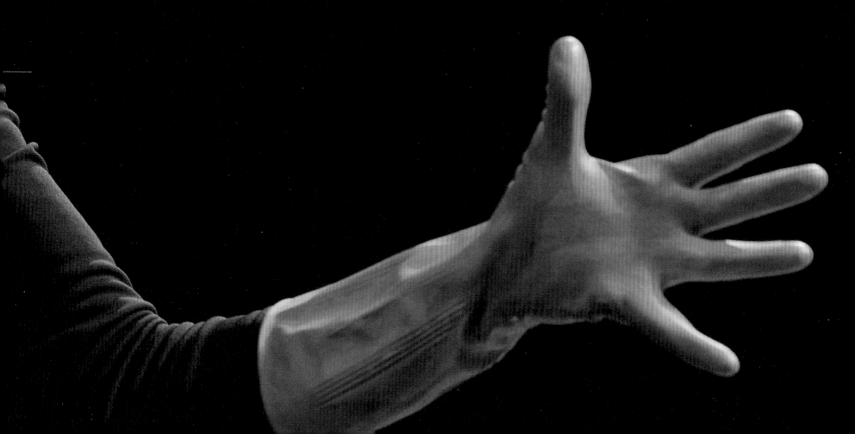

CAROLYN CARLSON

Double Vision, 2009, a cooperation between Carolyn Carlson and architects and artists Naziha Mestaoui and Yacine Aït Kaci (Electronic Shadow)

CAROLYN CARLSON

contemporary dance choreographer, performer, poet

What do you do? I breathe._____You say that it was learning from the choreographer Alwin Nikolaïs that made everything come together for you. How did this happen? It was the way he was working. For example, he would give a class on 'time passing'; you had to do something that would give a sense of time passing to the spectator. We did one-hour improvisations, during which each dancer worked on the same principle. With Nikolaïs, I have discovered the beauty of improvising on a theme. I found that improvisation was my pure nature. I am very spontaneous, that's why I like to do calligraphy. I do poetry concerts, improvisations, I work with jazz musicians. Twice a week, we'd also have composition focused on a specific theme, working in-depth on a certain principle, exploring the different qualities of an emotion. Let's take suspension: in class, we would explore suspension points, the suspension vertical, suspension by a finger, suspension by a hip . . . We would improvise on this with Nikolaïs criticising where we were wrong, and then we did a composition based on this, which was not improvised. The great thing about Nikolaïs was that he never went from A to B; you started with a point and followed a line. It was like creating poetry, and so it had a form, an inner structure. I still follow this method. Working on the solo piece for Diana, *Woman in a Room*, I got several poems by Arseny Tarkovsky, Andrei Tarkovsky's father. I asked Diana to choose one and improvise on what it meant to her. I said to her: "I don't want to know you as a dancer, I want to know who you are from inside, as a poet." Before we got to the technique, I worked with Diana as a woman on a poetry level. I was also inspired by Andrei Tarkovsky's films *Mirror* and *Sacrifice*, by his silence. People can watch that burning house in *Mirror* forever; it's like medita-

On stage, you are not *performing* , you TRANSCEND.

The ego disappears **; you** disappear **; because you** <u>are</u> **the form**

tion. You know what I love about solos? You share your loneliness; we are all lonely in a good sense._____Each day is new; you don't know what is going to happen. Each day something inspires you: you meet a person, you read a book, or you read a word. You can choreograph life. What's interesting about dance is the fact that it lives and dies in a second. It has to be precise, conscious and aware. Of course, there are films and photographs, but they would never replace a live performance. You can't write a book about dance; teaching is the only way to perpetuate a movement. Dance is transparent, it's vacant; it's a spiritual body form. When I do a movement, it happens right now and is never going to happen again. To me, dance is like life. We have to acknowledge our presence every moment. Again, it's like meditation: are we present in everything we do? That's the beauty of dance: you are present.

(pages 254–5, 257) <u>Woman in a Room</u>, a solo piece created for Diana Vishneva, 2013

According to Diana, it has been a revelatory experience, in the sense that she had learned a lot about herself. The kinds of things she has never been aware of. Art *is* therapy—and the public has to participate, to think. In classical ballets like *Swan Lake*, you are watching a solo and you can't really go inside the story, because the entire story is already there. This is why I love contemporary dance, which is very Zen, in a way. You make a suggestion; you do something that has to be imperfect, and it's the spectators that complete the picture using their own imagination. For me, it's about their beauty, too._____On stage, you transcend. Diana is not performing: she *is* this. If you are performing, your head is 'out here', but if you do the act, you *are* the form. Nikolaïs has introduced this idea of transcendence. We danced in sacks, so you couldn't see anything. All you could do was make shapes, but you couldn't see the faces. I had come from classical ballet, which is very much about 'look at me, I am beautiful'. Nikolaïs's main principle was transcending in act, in which you became humble. I work a lot on presence; that's something I got from martial arts. Nikolaïs always talked about the vertical, and later, taking tai chi classes, I realised that it was standing between Heaven and Earth. And when you hold your arms, you think of the horizon—you become infinite._____**What is the most challenging aspect of dance?** The awareness. You cannot lose one minute of concentration. It's physical, mental and spiritual work. I'm still doing a solo based on Mark Rothko's art. I've got a thousand people out there; it's an amazing responsibility. I know that the piece works, but it's a challenge. I have to be in form, in the moment. Every night is different. It's a risk. That's what is incredible about live performance: it's direct._____Kazuo Ohno, the Butoh dancer, said that, before he stepped on stage, he thought of the ancestors—which I do, too. I am a choreographer, I created a form, but where do I come from? I think of all those people who have come before me—Isadora Duncan, Mary Wigman, Alwin Nikolaïs—all of us come from someone, everyone has a Master. We can't forget them. I am part of a lineage, I'm in a line._____**Don't you think that any kind of creative work is a way to exteriorise your vision, to render your worldview 'visible' to other people?** It's about sharing. Dance is an incredible means of sending energy out. Why do we create? Because we want to share.

to bring together
what life has separated

perception without word
an eye without a tongue

a soul that moves
listens to a call

the act of completion
fusion in a spiritual
body form

poetry
in a glimpse of infinity

words and calligraphy by Carolyn Carlson

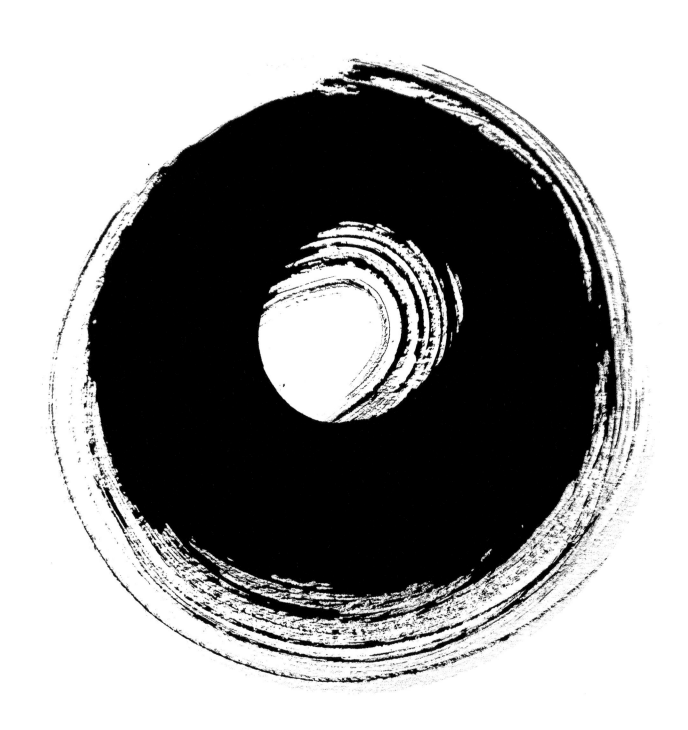

MANIFESTO

I

As a cosmological theory and as a book, MULTIVERSE celebrates the idea that our (personal) universe is not all there is to this world. The tantalising knowledge that other universes exist but can't be reached is not exclusive to cosmology, though. Every living being sees the world differently; sometimes—in a radically different way, and, at least for now, we are unable to experience someone else's reality._____The truly mind-blowing fact, however, is that the 'real' reality is all of these individual realities living and breathing together. Simultaneously. Here and now. All-in-one._____Art is here to testify this, and to attempt the impossible: reach out to the parallel worlds; hack other realities; create and share experiences. It is here to keep awake our sense of wonder.

II

Bauhaus visionary László Moholy-Nagy saw one of his generation's tasks as learning to live an integrated life. The life in which we would "function to the fullest of our capacities" because our intellect and emotions would finally start acting as a balanced whole. We will learn to "feel what we know and know what we feel".

Each historic period comes complete with an art that reflects a contemporary vision of the world. Art evolves together with this vision, and at times boldly fore-runs scientific insights._____Science is a human attempt to understand how the world functions. Art is an attempt to give back to the world what we have understood about it._____Science is about distinguishing music where there seems to be noise. It's when we recognise the existence of a code behind the apparent chaos and, ultimately, unravel it—but only to realise that this game, too, has still further levels. Art takes this code and turns it into a language—a living and therefore evolving system, in which every symbol unpacks into multiple meanings. We need this language so that we can share our discoveries with the world.

III

Charles Sirato's Dimensionalist Manifesto was written in 1936 and signed, among others, by Hans Arp, Marcel Duchamp, Robert and Sonia Delaunay and Vassily Kandinsky. The Dimensionalists argued that, with the new concept of time and space emerging in mathematics and physics, and the technology advancing at a rapid pace, arts, too, were acquiring new, extra dimensions. Accepting, either intuitively or consciously, that time and space are not separate but related categories, they saw "all the old borders and barriers of the arts disappear"._____Pushing this mindset even further, the Manifesto foresaw a completely new art form, defined as 'cosmic art', in which matter will merge with music, and artists will conquer four-dimensional space. "Rather than looking at art objects", the human being will become "the centre and the subject of the creative process that will consist of controlled sensory effects within a closed cosmic space".

IV

80 years later . . ._____The knowledge gained by the humanity over the past decades brings us before the world's breathtaking complexity and interconnectedness. Communication technologies are warping time and space on a daily basis. Cross-boundary, interdisciplinary thinking is becoming a matter or survival._____Today, an artist can only work in the presence of this knowledge. It's an awareness that cannot be 'unlearned'—and, as the mind's spotlight gets continuously adjusted, it keeps reminding us how big and profound the still unanswered questions are._____Overwhelmingly multi-dimensional, the contemporary vision of the world can hardly be expressed through the language of any single art. The quest, therefore, is for a new kind of language, the one that would be adequate to the constantly updated and therefore constantly reshaped vision. This new language will emerge from the synthesis of arts, but also (and no less importantly) from the synthesis of art with various branches of science and technology.

V

As scientific theories become increasingly complex, these new forms of art are perhaps the best way for us lay people to make sense of this newly acquired knowledge and of the way it changes our concept of reality._____Art has its own ways of delivering the message. Joining forces with technology that continues to expand the limits of what is possible, it radically expands our vision of the world. In doing so, it sparks not only our sense of wonder, but also the realisation that we can interact with this wonder, and that—just because we are witnessing it happen—we are already transforming and therefore co-creating it.

VI

Starting his work, the master builder of a Gothic cathedral knew there was no chance for him to see the project completed. He didn't even have a drawing of what the end result would look like. But, while the construction works were still in progress, the cathedral would already function. A magnificent piece of art in the making, a major nucleus of the city life, and . . . shall we say a living organism, almost?_____Today, when the concept of time and space undergoes radical transformation, which newly added dimensions will enable the 'cosmic art' predicted by the Dimensionalists? Given that neither time nor space 'really' exists, what kind of art would be capable of speaking for an eternal *now* that comprises all *heres* at once? Will it be an art that, just like a cathedral, arises from many cooperating efforts to become a synergy of multiple realities? Will it incorporate the audience in the making-of process? And will it offer constant change as a never-final outcome?

IMAGE CREDITS

DIANA VISHNEVA
Irina Grigoryeva 5
Alex Gouliaev 6, 12–3 (10), 14, 20, 61, 174–5
Irina Tuminene 8, 260–1
Mark Olich 17, 18, 122–3
Nikolay Krusser 22–3, 269
BAIACEDEZ 2014 / photo: Sylvain Gouraud 236–7, 266

CARLO RATTI
Ian Ehm 26–7 (10), 30
Nicholas Ruhlmann, Wyatt Burns 28 (top), 29
Pietro Leoni 28 (bottom)
Lucas Werthein 32 (top left)
MyBossWas 33 (top)
Adam Pruden 32 (bottom left)
Daniel McDuff, MIT 32 (bottom right)
Sanders Hernandez, CMYK+WHITE 33 (bottom)
Ramak Fazel 35

TOYO ITO
Courtesy of Toyo Ito & Associates 36–7 (10, 38)
Kai Nakamura 40
Ishiguro Photographic Institute 41 (top)
Courtesy of Toyo Ito & Associates / photo: Iwan Baan 41 (bottom)

FRANCIS KURKDJIAN
Nathalie Baetens 42–3 (10, 44), 45–6
Courtesy of Maison Francis Kurkdjian 49

PHILIPPE RAHM
Jérôme Schlomoff 50–1 (10, 54)
Courtesy of Philippe Rahm Architectes 52 (top)
Nicolas Pauly 52 (bottom)
Brøndum & Co 53
Adam Rzepka / Centre Pompidou 56
Michel Legendre 57
Niklaus Stauss 59 (top)
Jean-Michel Landecy 59 (bottom)

ANGELIN PRELJOCAJ
Lucas Marquand Perrier 62–3 (10, 64)
Alex Gouliaev 66, 67
Nikolay Krusser 69

JOHN NEUMEIER
Steven Haberland 70–1 (10, 74)
Irina Grigoryeva 72–3
Nikolay Krusser 76–7, 79
Irina Tuminene 80–1

ROSS LOVEGROVE
Courtesy of Lovegrove Studio

IRIS VAN HERPEN
Ioulux 94–5 (10, 99)
Morgan O'Donovan 96 (top)
Michel Zoeter 96 (bottom), 100–1
Ingrid Baars 97
Robert Clark 103

ENKI BILAL
Courtesy of Enki Bilal 104–5 (10, 106)
Enki Bilal – Casterman 108
Enki Bilal 109–10

CARSTEN NICOLAI
All artworks by the artist © Carsten Nicolai, by SIAE
2017 / VG Bildkunst Bonn
Sebastian Mayer 112–13 (10, 116)
Richard-Max Tremblay 114-15, 119 (top left)
Courtesy Galerie EIGEN+ART Leipzig/Berlin and
Pace Gallery / photo: Julija Stankeviciene 118,
Uwe Walter 119 (top right), 121 (top),
Carsten Nicolai 119 (bottom), 121 (bottom)

MARCO GOECKE
Nadja Kadel 124–5 (10, 128)
Irina Grigoryeva 126–7, 130
Irina Tuminene 131, 133

BILL VIOLA
Courtesy of Bill Viola Studio

SANTIAGO CALATRAVA
Michael Falco 146–7 (11, 148)
Rem Khass 150–1, 153

MIGUEL CHEVALIER
Courtesy of Miguel Chevalier

AES+F
Dina Shedrinskaya 165 (11, 169)
Courtesy of AES+F 166–7, 170–1, 173

EDOUARD LOCK
Courtesy of Edouard Lock 176–7 (11, 178)
Nikolay Krusser 180, 181 (bottom)
Alex Gouliaev 181 (top), 183

MOSES PENDLETON
Moses Pendleton 184–5 (11, 188), 186, 190
Nina Alovert 187, 191
Gene Schiavone 193

AITOR THROUP
Charles Moriarty 196–7 (11, 200)
Neil Bedford 198, 203 (top), 205
Courtesy of Aitor Throup Studio 199, 202

OLAFUR ELIASSON
Courtesy of Studio Olafur Eliasson 206–7 (11, 210)
Anna Yudina 208 (top)
Courtesy of Louis Vuitton Malletier, Paris, France
© Olafur Eliasson / photo: Studio Olafur Eliasson 208
(bottom)
Courtesy of the artist; neugerriemschneider, Berlin;
Tanya Bonakdar Gallery, New York © Olafur Eliasson /
photo: Anders Sune Berg 209, 213, Olafur Eliasson 215
Courtesy of Aros Aarhus Kunstmuseum, Denmark
© Olafur Eliasson / photo: Studio Olafur Eliasson 212

RAFFAELLO D'ANDREA
Zurich.Minds 216–17
Edith Paol 11, 220
Nichola Feldman-Kiss 218
Carolina Flores, ETH Zurich 219, 222 (bottom)
François Lauginie 223
Sparked Team 225

NICK KNIGHT
Jon Emmony / SHOWstudio 226 (11, 230)
Courtesy of Nick Knight / SHOWstudio 228–9, 232–3,
235

WILLIAM FORSYTHE
Dominik Mentzos 238–9 (11, 242), 240, 244, 247
Vladimir Lupovskoy 241, 245 (top)
Valentin Baranovsky 245 (bottom)

CAROLYN CARLSON
Laurent Paillier / photosdedanse.com 248–9 (11, 252)
Courtesy of Electronic Shadow 250–1
Nikolay Krusser 254–5, 257 (bottom right)
Jerry Metellus 257 (top and bottom left)
Carolyn Carlson 259

GRAVITATION: VARIATION IN TIME AND SPACE
Courtesy of the filmmakers

GRAVITATION :
variation in time and space

A sample of *multiversal* art, the experimental film *Gravitation: Variation in Time and Space* is a synergy of dance, cinema, and state-of-the-art technology. Directed by Andrei Severny and based on the original idea of the producer Rem Khass, *Gravitation* brings together Mauro Bigonzetti's choreographic work, Diana Vishneva's performance and Steve Romano's Phantom Flex4K camera to deconstruct the language of dance and translate it into that of cinema. Through the calligraphy of black and white images, it explores the notions of time and space, movement and light. "We tried to show a ballerina's movement like you have never seen it before. Powerful back lighting and slow motion focuses the viewers' attention on the perfection of the lines and guides them into a striking visual world. The shots of the Moon and space from the NASA archives become metaphors of loneliness and the eternity of space, and make us reconsider the entire notion of time," Severny comments on this story of creation, inner struggle and transformation.

Author and designer: Anna Yudina

Acknowledgements:
Vladimir Smirnov Foundation
Rem Khass

5 CONTINENTS EDITIONS
Editorial Coordination: Laura Maggioni
Art Direction: Annarita De Sanctis
Translation: Caroline Higgitt
Editing: Emily Ligniti
Colour Separation: Maurizio Brivio, Italy

ISBN 978-88-7439-779-2

Front cover:
Diana Vishneva in *Tué*
Choreographer: Marco Goecke
Photo: Irina Grigoryeva

5 Continents Editions
Piazza Caiazzo 1
20124 Milan, Italy
www.fivecontinentseditions.com

DVD:
Gravitation: Variation in Time and Space
Key cast and crew:
Principal Dancer: Diana Vishneva
Choreographer: Mauro Bigonzetti
Director and Editor: Andrei Severny
Producer; original idea: Rem Khass
Director of Photography: Steve Romano
© Diana Vishneva Foundation

Distributed in the United States and Canada
by Harry N. Abrams, Inc., New York
Distributed outside the United States and Canada,
excluding France, Italy and South America,
by Yale University Press, London

Printed and bound in Italy in June 2017
by Tecnostampa – Pigini Group Printing Division Loreto – Trevi, Italy,
for 5 Continents Editions, Milan